DATE DUE

NOV 5	1981		
MAY 3 '82	Motter		
MAY 20	1983		
MAR 11	1985		
APR 08 RECD	Spordell		
MAY 07 1988	Paper	MAY 05 PAID	
NOV 03 1992		NOV 0 3 RECD	
GAYLORD			PRINTED IN U.S.A.

Nigerian Modernization

The Colonial Legacy

Nigerian Modernization
The Colonial Legacy

Ukandi Godwin Damachi

Princeton University

With a Foreword
by Wilbert E. Moore
University of Denver

The Third Press

Joseph Okpaku Publishing Company, Inc.
444 Central Park West, New York, N.Y. 10025

Library of Congress Catalogue Card Number: 75-183394

SBN 89388-030-2

Designed by Bennie Arrington

Printed in the U.S.A.   First Printing

In Memory of My Beloved Sister,
Rosaline Ishi Damachi

ACKNOWLEDGMENT

My obligations are numerous and some of the heaviest must remain unacknowledged. I am indebted to Professor Bernard Karsh, both my academic and thesis adviser, for his guidance and direction, and to Professors Allan Peshkin and Walter Franke for reading through the first draft of my thesis and for the valuable advice they rendered. My appreciation and thanks also go to all the Professors in the Institute of Labor and Industrial Relations especially, Professor William E. Chalmers, for their patience and interest in my work.

My acknowledgment also goes to the Saint Patrick's Missionary Order in Ireland for their kindness and their help to me while I was there as well as their continuing interest in me here in the United States.

I am indebted to my parents for the early stages of my education as well as my two uncles, Mr. John U. Odey and Mr. Joseph A. Agba for the help and advice given to me all through my stay in Champaign-Urbana.

Special thanks to Anice Duncan for her cooperation and help in time of need. Also sincere thanks to Edmund S. Egozi, Christopher Ikediobi, and Daphne Talbot for the encouragement they gave to me during the most difficult periods of this work.

I also wish to acknowledge the valuable work by Madeline D. Spitaleri and Patricia Burcham who did the typing. Without their assistance it would have been impossible to make the date-line.

Finally I offer my genuine appreciation to Professor Neil J. Smelser of Berkeley and Professor Alfred Opubor who offered valuable suggestions after reading the first draft.

Contents

FOREWORD
Wilbert E. Moore

When this study was undertaken and the first draft of the report completed, Nigeria was torn by civil war. Or, if one wants to be more precise, it was torn by a war of secession, the truncated national government in Lagos attempting to put down the rebellious independence of the proclaimed Republic of Biafra. Damachi was studying abroad during most of the conflict (in Ireland and the United States) and was a colleague of mine at the Russell Sage Foundation in New York when it ended. Knowing my own interest in comparative studies of labor systems, Damachi sought my advice on the possible publication of the study now at hand. My initial reaction was one of admiration for the report and analysis, including the commendable style of exposition, but tempered optimism about publication. A conspicuous difficulty was that at the time Nigeria was newsworthy mainly because of the Biafran secession and the war, and on this Damachi's manuscript was silent. When I challenged him on this, his position was that the war was likely to be a transitory historical circumstance, whatever its outcome, and despite the devastation, human suffering, and probably lasting animosities. The outcome, he argued, would change the basic structure of social and labor relations only in details, important to participants but not seriously affecting the general patterns.

The final defeat of the Biafran secession did indeed occur rather quickly. And although it would be improper to assume Nigerian national unity—regionalism and tribalism remain serious problems and will continue to influence the organization and disposition of productive manpower—the author's attempt to analyze and appraise social and labor relations at a more general and more enduring level has been vindicated.

Damachi's study is that of a "new nation," thought by many to have an unusually good chance for a relatively smooth transition from colonialism to a viable democracy. Nigeria, however, is a large country in both area and population, and its regions are different in language, tribal organization and customs, religion, and "culture" not elsewhere classified. Now the "multi-communal" nation is the most common circumstance of new nations, but also of many old and orderly democracies: witness Belgium, Netherlands, Switzerland, the United Kingdom, and the United States. New nations have also an additional problem: the relations between a native élite developed under the colonial regime, and the new élite that is likely to emerge in the post-colonial era. Since the British colonial policy in West Africa was that of "indirect rule," there was in Nigeria both a continuity with tribal leadership (which was invented where it was not fully established) and some development of a modern civil service.

Despite all difficulties, modernization in Nigeria has been going on rapidly. Indeed, in the form of urbanization, the pace of change outstrips the expansion of urban facilities and of regularized employment in the modernized sector of the economy. In this respect, too, Nigeria suffers a common fate with other modernizing countries. What remains to be seen, there and elsewhere, is whether the various social divisions of the population that existed before colonial rule, those established as part of the colonial legacy, and those typical of urban-industrial societies can be accommodated in a social order that is simultaneously singular and plural. Damachi's conclusion is also one of tempered optimism.

For those scholars not totally caught up in campus riots, national politics, or other forms of insanity, this book represents an outstanding example of the merits of attempting to detect the broader significance of social change caught while it is in process.

Damachi is black and I am white and to complicate matters he is Catholic and I am Protestant (if anything). We have a common calling, however; we share an enthusiasm for dispassionate social analysis. There must be a moral in this, somewhere.

Nigerian Modernization

The Colonial Legacy

I

INTRODUCTION

The tendency toward industrialization and urbanization, which is both directly and indirectly due to the action of the colonists, is one of the outstanding characteristics of present-day life in Nigeria. The causes of this tendency are not all of recent origin, but its acceleration is recent. Indeed the colonial situation involves not only intervention and the introduction of new techniques and cultural models, the appearance of new processes of social differentiation; it entails with respect to that dominant minority which is the "foreign elite," a reorientation of the social structure. In overcoming the traditional equilibriums, it sets a chain of radical social change into motion.

In order for the colonial masters to administer the colony, it was necessary to orientate the Nigerians toward Western values. This resulted in a drastic shift from the traditional to the Western values. As a result, traditional social institutions were disequilibriated and in their place modern ones were being instituted. In fact, the colonial contact initiated a lot of social processes unknown to traditional Nigeria, especially processes of differentiation and integration. With differentiation there was a modification of the traditional social institutions while new ones (economic, governmental, educational) sprang up. Traditional beliefs and religion, family structure and functions, social stratification and traditional associations were all affected.

At the same time, the establishment of European control brought about a dislocation of the native populations, which has had more far reaching consequences than native wars and the slave trade. It has radically changed the physical basis of life for large sections of the native population.

3

There has been industrialization of agriculture through the development of plantations. Included in the same category are the large-scale schemes for commercial crops, as, for example, cacao and groundnut. Although originally the farming of these two crops was carried on by small farm owners, large plantations with tenants have gradually come into existence. The effect of industrialization on the native populations is even more striking wherever mining has been introduced in Nigeria—this results in a wage-earning labor force and urban centers. The corollary of these two results is the process of urbanization which causes an influx into the towns which very often overstrains the labor market and the local economy, and thus helps to increase insecurity. And insecurity is causing great anxiety in official circles since it is affecting an ever-increasing proportion of the total population. Concomitant with the inception and development of educational and political institutions has been a related change, or rather evolution, in social structure. As political growth has been largely brought about by the activities of the small educated elite, mutations in the social system have been equally the by-product of education and Westernization.

The gradual substitution of new status values for the old in the areas most exposed to British rule had an infectious effect. A Nigerian elite modeled on European lines has been in the process of formation. At first the Africans who helped the colonizers to build the new colonial structure were mainly from older British possessions in Sierra Leone and Ghana; the townsmen of Lagos and other localities were brought in later and eventually came to supplant the outsiders as clerks, teachers, and in other occupations where literacy was a requisite.

The expansion of this nucleus of British-trained Nigerians was largely the result of missionary efforts. Years later, Nigerians began to go overseas, principally to Great Britain, to obtain higher education. Succeeding generations were more self-assertive, competitive and ambitious; their leaders sought more aggressively to clear the path to advancement. This Westernized elite is now responsible for guiding Nigeria's destiny. It is youthful, well-educated, following urban living patterns on the European model, with Christian—or less usually Moslem—religious affiliation, and profoundly conscious and proud of Nigeria, without losing sight of the sectional interests with which their political affiliations to a large extent automatically identify them.

So far we have seen some of the vast social changes which industrialization and Westernization, by-products of colonialism, have brought about. As a result of this, I am going to assume that industrialization started at the inception of colonialism.

If we accept this assumption, then a wide spectrum of social change within the traditional institutions is open to us. In this instance, therefore, the question of focus becomes vital. The present study is focused upon effects of colonialism and its concomitants (industrialization, Westernization) on some of the outstanding traditional institutions and values. Accordingly, therefore, stress will be laid on colonial and industrializing effects on the traditional values, beliefs and religion; rural-urban migration, political organization and its influence on industrialization and modernization; and since the "elites" are the forerunners and the promoters of political organization, a chapter dealing with their aspirations, characteristics, problems and weaknesses becomes necessary to understand the whole process of industrialization which they are bent on promoting.

A question may be raised why I limit myself to these four social aspects of industrialization. Nigeria is far the largest and most populous country in Africa. It is the twelfth most populous in the world. It contains within its borders the three largest nationalities in Africa—each numbering more than five million. Moreover, the groups that make up its population reflect the widest range of political organization as well as the widest range of beliefs and values of any nation in Africa. It is the only political entity in Africa where most of the main African language groups, religious groups, ethnic and racial groups are found. In short, in terms of size and diversity Nigeria has much to distinguish it from other countries.

These very features—Nigeria's immense size and its complex diversity—coupled with the fact that this study is exploratory, have dictated several sharp delimitations. But as a matter of focus, I have to narrow it to the four areas mentioned above. A look at the gradual value change is vital for several social scientists today, notably ethnographers and social anthropologists. It will stress the importance of recognizing "Westernization" as a relative and partial process which took place in differing contexts alongside a persistence, in varying degrees, of traditional habits and values. For this reason a careful study of the character and foundations of traditional values and of the influence they had on the assimilation and modification of "Western" attitudes is necessary both among the peoples of the towns and among the tribal populations from which they had been drawn. This point is again relevant while discussing the social relationship between urban and rural populations and the psychological and economic consequences of the growing dichotomy between tribal and urban ways of life. The need for intensive inquiry into cultural patterning and social institutions is also being recognized. Not only are such studies necessary in themselves, but they are usually indispensable prerequisites for the framing of an adequate "social survey" and the interpretation of results. The study could open the way for social surveys of this kind:

1. Problems of assessing values and motivations in tribal and urban societies in Africa; the adaptation of psychological tests to non-literate and semi-literate populations; the analysis and systematization of field data provided from observation and verbal statements.
2. The character and diversity of pre-existing value patterns among Nigerian populations.
3. Symbolic significance of (a) traditional and (b) Western patterns of behavior and the new social differentiation expressed therein.
4. Conflict of values and their effects on social solidarity, reliability in work and social cooperation.

Rural-urban migration is important because of the forms industrialization has taken in Nigeria. There are four principal forms whose relative importance differs from one area to another: the introduction of mining, leading to the settling of labor in company camps or villages near the mining area; the development of plantations, involving the employment of large numbers of seasonal workers; the large-scale development of industrial crops grown by small Nigerian farmers with Nigerian hired labor—e.g., cacao, cotton; and finally the development of transport, factory industries and commerce, leading to the growth of a diversified wage-earning class, of which a proportion, differing considerably from one area to another, is settled permanently in towns. Most sociological research which has given, or plans to give, information on the effects of these developments has been done in urban areas. So a comparison of rural and urban life will help to draw attention to rural research also. Normally, the social effects of development fall into two broad groups: those resulting from the creation of a heterogeneous, largely unskilled, partly illiterate, wage-earning population in towns, and those resulting from the temporary or permanent absence of young men and women from tribal areas. These two aspects are, of course, part of the land problem and I raise it in the study.

In the advanced industrial nations, industrialization was brought about by the working or middle classes but in the developing nations it is the work of the different governments concerned. Industrialization is therefore promoted by political organization. As a result of this a chapter is devoted to considering the influence of political organization on the process of industrialization and modernization.

But to talk of political organization is to talk of the new "Western elites" who are the dynamic force behind any government action; they are the decision- and policy-makers. So to adequately understand industrialization in developing countries, one has to understand the elitist class in that country. For this reason, I shall consider the characteristics of the "elites."

On the whole the importance of the study becomes more apparent if we consider the fact that the UNESCO conference on "Social Implications of Industrialization and Urbanization in Africa South of the Sahara," stresses the same effects as my study.

> The study of the social conditions of industrialization and urbanization should be mainly focused on the analysis of social processes and of individual and collective behavior with reference to the reconstructing of urban life.
>
> It is hoped that particular attention would be paid to: (a) religious institutions and the new values and motivations that are emerging within the various categories; (b) the degree of mutual integration of groups of different ethnic origin and social status; (c) the effects of education, wider knowledge and experience at all levels upon the integration of urban communities; (d) the facilities afforded in this field by industrial concerns.[1]

As a matter of approach to the study, I shall take the traditional Nigerian society as a dependent variable. Since I have assumed that industrialization is a concomitant of colonialism, I shall take both of them as independent variables to be introduced to the dependent variable (the traditional society). I shall then note changes which have taken place as a result of the collision of the dependent and independent variables. Attempts will be made to show the rate of assimilation, resistance and modification by the traditional sector as each of the social aspects chosen is discussed. This calls for a summary of the major changes at the end of each chapter. As a conclusion, I shall try to expose the interchange system which has resulted between traditionality and colonialism (industrialization, modernization), that is, what the traditional society has gained from and lost to colonialism and vice versa.

II
CHANGE IN THE VALUE SYSTEM: THE EFFECTS OF THIS ON:

The Nigerian society, which was characteristic of traditionality, is under a transition to modernization. This shift towards modernization and industrialization gives rise to many radical changes in the culture. There tends to be a conflict between the indigenous culture and the Western. The educated tilt more to the Western culture while the illiterate majority, especially the old generation, insist on tradition. With this crossroad, there have been changes in beliefs and religion, family structure and its functions, social stratification and the Nigerian has acquired a new personality. Most of these changes in the system still retain some of the basic traditional values like extended family.

Since Nigeria achieved political independence, she has strived for true economic self-direction. But unfortunately, current rates of growth of output do not satisfy the aspirations of nationalist political leaders, partly for material, partly for cultural, and partly for political reasons. On the material level they are conscious of the poverty of the great mass of Nigerians and of everything that goes with poverty—poor nutrition, poor housing, high infant mortality rates, and the like. Instead of a war on poverty, the elite now give priority to higher standards—water systems, electricity, paved roads, home industries, better transportation and communications, greater efficiency of labor. These and other economic aims require more capital and more efficient organization for getting anticipated results. If the elite feel frustrated by their inability to achieve these goals quickly, they are likely to increase their emphasis on central planning, precedent for which is the government corporation system of economic development inherited from colonial days.[1] Potential investment by foreign entrepreneurs or governments is sub-

9

stantially curtailed by policy growing from the elite's determination to manage Nigeria's affairs without external domination.[2]

Much is made in nationalist circles of African art and music, but Nigerians (Africans as a whole) are conscious that their music is as great an artistic achievement as that of Beethoven, that they have oral literature which is long standing, that their religions are on rather a high level, and that their kinship and other social patterns, which are such a joy to the anthropologist, have been unwittingly and grossly distorted by the so-called Africanists. Beyond all this, Nigerians want material progress because they wish to be recognized as living on standards as high as any other people. The reasons here suggested may not be the driving reasons, and, if they are, they may be false, in the sense that material progress may not bring any of the things which Nigerians or Africans in general really want. In fact, it is likely to bring about alienation of her citizens and a breakdown of their familial ties. However this may be, there is no doubt that the hearts of the new political leaders are set upon material progress. The old leaders, the chiefs and traditional authorities, do not all share this outlook, and, as one moves from modern towns into remoter villages, it is shared less and less by the masses of the people themselves. But this is nevertheless a challenge which the Nigerian rulers have to meet in all their political relations with the new Nigerian. These political relations will be developed further in a later chapter.[3]

Other new values include acquisitiveness and social mobility. As Nigerians succeeded expatriates in positions of leadership and responsibility, they took over the living quarters which accompanied high positions and moved at the same time into patterns of affluence in living standards. The struggle to improve one's status in society, which has grown with increasing Westernization, was strengthened. Above all, Nigerian leaders trained abroad in acquisitive societies set an example of accumulation of wealth. Any corruption by the personal acquisition of wealth could be rationalized as the price of getting Nigeria ready to handle her own affairs with the outside world. Obtaining Nigerian control of what had once been the prerogative of foreign investors seemed to be as much a patriotic necessity as a matter of private advancement.[4]

Social Values According to Ethnic Groups

There are some distinctive sets of social values which characterize the various ethnic groups. In all regions of Nigeria, there are contrasts between rural and urban values. In the Moslem North, town dwellers are more thoroughly Islamized and look down on country folk, including pastoral Fulani, for being less observant in faith[5] (this idea will be developed when discussing religion).[6] In the South, urban-rural differences are not acute among the Yoruba, but in other ethnic groups, whole traditional backgrounds are entirely rural, and rapid twentieth century urbanization, tied to Western enterprise and education, is associated with a shift in values over which there is some degree of conflict between migrants and their rural relatives. Throughout Southern urban areas, the Pidgin-English adjective "bush" is commonly applied to rural areas and used to ridicule unsophisticated migrants bringing rustic ways to the city. Frequently, the epithet is pugnaciously resented. Both in the Moslem and Semi-Moslem North and in semi-Westernized South, townsmen scorn country people as ignorant fools, and country people may retaliate with a stereotype of townsmen as swindlers.[7]

Among exposing value systems, rooted in the past, most powerful is that of Islam linked to the Northern emirate system. On the whole, the emirate areas in Nigeria have been kept insulated from Western influences, so that the Moslem emphasis on submission to authority and the historic forms of state authority in the Moslem North are hardly yet faced with extensive democratic challenge on their home ground.[8] There is an almost oriental flavor to the deference shown by the Hausa to their superiors in the highly formalized social hierarchy.

In the far North, democratic values of equal opportunity and open competition are still new and not widely accepted as valid inspirations. Emphasis is rather on maintaining reverent submission to the traditional inequalities. An individual is encouraged to enhance his personal position by hard work, through which as a craftsman and trader he may become relatively prosperous. Prestige is accorded to religious knowledge, which may be gained through study under a "Mallam" [9] and to pious observance of the wide range of Moslem religious requirements for a virtuous life, such as daily prayers and dietary restrictions, including absention from alcohol. The conservative values of the "holy North" are reflected in the motto chosen for the Northern Region's coat of arms, "Work and Worship." [10]

The nomadic pastoral Fulani are sharply set apart from the settled agricultural Hausa. As a people whose immemorial way of life has been to follow shifting migratory circuits from pasture to pasture, superficially encountering diverse other peoples en route, the pastoral Fulani has a strongly entrenched concern to safeguard their own values by defining them in an explicit code (pulsaku, "the Fulani way") and proudly emphasize their aloofness from outsiders with contrasting ways. They scorn cultivator's work with a hoe, prize the possession of cattle, partly because of the very fact that it distinguishes them from neighboring peoples, and consider the loss of herds the gravest of misfortunes.[11] To them the modern values mentioned above mean little or nothing. As far as they are concerned, transition from the traditional to the modern ways of life is almost absent and where it exists at all, it is painfully slow.

By comparison with the Fulanis, the Ibos are less respectful of formal organization and static class barriers, largely because of the democratic tendency in traditional Ibo social values. The Ibos do not believe in paternalism; rather the achievement ethic is paramount. They are very individualistic.

Ottenberg writing on the social values and attitudes of the Ibos reported that: "The Ibo are a highly individualistic people. While a man is dependent on his family, lineage, and residential grouping for support and backing, strong emphasis is placed on his ability to make his own way in the world." [13] A man can become rich through the skillful use of the farming resources of his friends and relatives, trade, and use of loans. The attainment of wealth means the attainment of prestige and influence, through respect, clientage, assumption of titles, and achievement of political influence. The competitive pattern in life is further manifested in rivalry among villages and other lineage groups for size, wealth, and influence.

Leadership in Ibo society is not merely a question of seniority, but is dependent on an elder's knowledge of village and compound history and affairs, wealth, demonstrated capacity as a leader, ability to speak clearly, persuasively, and without offending others, and interest in local affairs.

Emphasis is placed on the equality of membership of a social group and of different social groups of a similar type. While differences in social rank and authority of course existed, there was a basic egalitarian attitude.[14]

The Yoruba remain more conservative in their values than the Ibo. They place a high value on age, and age-sets continue to act as the basic factor in the social structure.[15] Even educated Yoruba city dwellers follow the traditional practice of prostrating themselves before an elder member of their family or the families of their friends as a symbol of respect.

With regard to their pattern of government,[16] the head of the lineage is the eldest male, but the ruler of the kingdom is selected from a single royal lineage group. If the lineage head becomes unacceptable in his role of authority, he is not deposed. Another becomes the de facto head. If the king becomes unacceptable, he is asked to die. In each case, rule and decision by the head was a product of deliberation and consent by the representatives of the constituent groups of the corporate body.

The land was carefully developed to insure that it was always available to those who needed it and was kept in cultivation. Interests in land became increasingly well defined as the mode of settlement became more permanent, and land became scarce in relation to those who made claims for its use. The principle might be stated that, from the jural standpoint, lineage and individual interests in land multiplied and became more precise as a result of the permanency of settlement of land and increase in the numbers of users of land. The head of the lineage, the chief, and his advisors, each had their sphere of competence as they made decisions concerning the allocation and use of land among the members of the family, the community, and the kingdoms, respectively. The exercise of authority in such matters was not arbitrary but was a product of joint discussion and consensus in the relevant group or its representatives.[17]

Viewing Nigeria as a whole, there are some common elements. Prominent among them are the modern prestige of educational qualifications and their practical linkage with access to government employment or other profitable urban livelihoods which has had much to do with upsetting the traditional prestige of age and seniority. Young people have often become aggressively critical of their elders and riduculed their illiteracy and ignorance of the wider modern world. The new self-confidence and assertiveness of youth is based in part on the traditional value attached to superior wealth, since young migrant earners and holders of salaried urban positions, especially in government, are often much more prosperous than their stay-at-home rural elders. "Imported consumer goods, such as an automobile, are valued both for themselves and as outward signs of affluence and career success.[18]

The individual's values are becoming more recognized. For values accepted as part of each individual's own conception of what he should be and how he desires to live are initially inculcated during childhood experience in a kinship setting which is almost always broader and more complex than is family life in the Western world. The child is both deliberately and circumstantially trained in values of obedience and deference to elders, cooperation and sharing with age mates, making graded distinctions at all age levels in terms of exact seniority. There is nowhere an ideal of flat equality. The child learns very early to observe priorities among siblings in terms of their birth order, the relative seniority of their mothers in a polygamous household, and the priority of brothers over sisters. In case of polygamous families the ideals of cooperation and sharing are firmer between children of the same mother, than they are between children of different mothers but of the same father. Children are often made to be aware throughout their earliest years of the rivalry and spiteful intrigues between the mother and her co-wives, so that it becomes normal to be on guard in human relationships generally.[19]

The solidarity among close kinsmen and the individual's primary loyalty to those of his own home are extended more or less widely with milder and variable force to include more remote kin and members of the same tribe as a territorial and cultural unit. The series of loyalties with diminishing priorities from brothers, close cousins, and remoter cousins, to tribe, district, and region give rise to bitter internal jealousies, splitting along the lines of closer priorities, and possibly violent conflicts at any level (now at the national level which almost tore the country apart—that is, the civil war). At least up to the most extended level of acknowledged kinship, which in some instances is the entire tribe, factions tend to suspend their quarrels and draw together for mutual support and defense against any threat from persons less closely related or from complete outsiders. The Tiv provide an especially striking example of how loyalties and potential hostilities are apt to be graded in intensity.[20]

The high priority of kin solidarity and seniority discipline has been weakened somewhat among young people from parts of the coastal areas because of their education, new economic opportunities, and geographic mobility. They have often become noticeably more individualistic in their striving for success.[21] Among migrants the need for mutual help is met by organizations of those from the same locality, which reinforce sentiments and obligations of kinship. But these home-locality unions are being supplemented by political parties (which are of course momentarily banned by the military government) and other associations framed in less parochial terms.[22]

In the long run, as more and more migrant individuals commit themselves to living permanently in urban areas and as they rise in economic status, they become more interested in ideals of progress for a region of Nigeria as a whole, and they press for the establishment of secure rights and opportunities throughout the modern state for all citizens regardless of specific origin. The fundamental kinship logic which underlies exclusive tribal loyalties remains in force, and these precipitated the civil war.

In spite of the fact that people are quickly adopting these new values, the older generation distrusts many of the new values that have replaced the older ones such as emphasis on the use and sacredness of land, respect for elders, and fealty to the chief. They question, even as they succumb to it, the great stress on the acquisition of money and possessions, on the improvement of status, on the drive for education as means of attaining personal prestige and a larger income.[23]

Beliefs and Religion

Belief in supernatural powers is deeply ingrained in all parts of the country. The expression of belief follows the forms of numerous indigenous cult traditions or of Islam and Christianity, the two imported religions which have been replacing them. The 1953 census indicated that 44 per cent of the population was Moslem; 22 per cent Christian and 34 per cent other religions. However, there have been more converts since then.

Islam holds almost exclusive sway in the province along the northern border, known to Nigerian Moslems as the "Holy North" and has substantial footholds southward as far as the coast at the extreme southwest. Christianity's greatest strength is along the coast, primarily in the extreme southeast; it is influential in pockets northward through the central and eastern sections of the Middle Belt.[24]

The indigenous cults, commonly called "pagan," still prevail in the Eastern Middle Belt and in scattered rural areas of all the regions where people are most isolated from urban contacts and influences.[25] Almost everywhere rural pagans who have contacts with urban dwellers are gradually accepting Islam or Christianity and suppressing pagan observances to some extent. But since converts have seldom completely abandoned all the old local beliefs and ritual requirements there is, even in urban areas, an extensive overlap between persisting pagan religions and the claims of the two newer ones.

The pagan traditions, though no longer fully acknowledged in most places, continue to exert their influence on belief and behavior because they express intimate loyalties to birth-place and local group of kindred, a sacred community embracing the living and the dead. Each ethnic group has its own distinct religious traditions tied to sacred spots in its homeland. Usually their unwritten creeds and ritual systems require homage to the spirits of their dead ancestors and to personified forces of nature working the immediate locality, particularly the deity of the earth and its fertility. These spirits and deities, with their power to grant well-being or to visit misfortune, support systems of local usages, rights and obligations by which, supposedly, bygone generations had always lived. Frequently they support the political authority of a sacred king or priest-chief.[26]

The two imported religions, Islam and Christianity, have put old religions on the defensive because of their aggressive spread, but as I have previously mentioned, they continue to keep such an intimate hold on belief and behavior among so many nominal or partly converted Moslems and Christians that they still furnish the predominant religious influence for Nigeria as a whole. A convert may translate into more specific terms the spiritual theology and elevated ethical principles of the two world religions; yet he may continue to indulge in certain pagan rituals especially if he is dogged by difficulties.

Each pagan body of tradition acknowledges the existence of several types of supernatural entities apart from the spirit of ancestors and dead rulers. Personified forces of nature are approached ceremonially at prominent landmarks such as groves, hills, and streams, or at temples or shrines set up for them in the custody of priests or other dedicated persons. The most common of these deities is the earth, regarded as a god or goddess of fertility controlling agricultural activities, sometimes identified with the ultimate ancestors and concerned, as are all the ancestors, with general morality. Among the others are gods of war, of the sky and thunder, of iron, iron working, and of rivers, streams, and lagoons. A supreme deity who created all other deities and the world of men is frequently recognized, but this god usually has no emblems, shrines, or cult observances like the prayers and offerings of the other gods.[27]

The practices provide sacred expression for the feeling of having a common ancestry and of sharing a distinctive heritage of customs in communities attached to a particular territory. The cult of spirits of the dead is their most characteristic feature; in some instances it is emphatically the core of religion, in others it is less prominent. Each dwelling compound may contain shrines and sacrificial altars in addition to more important ones at sites shared by the whole village, township, or district. Various objects, often carved representations of the dead, are used as sacred symbols of supernatural powers; when chickens or other animals are sacrificed, the blood is poured upon these emblems. Millet beer, palm wine, or other liquids are poured upon the ground as offerings to the earth deity.[28]

The divergent traditional structures of political authority are matched and reinforced by corresponding religious tendencies. Where, as with the Ibo, governing authority is extensively divided among the members of local councils of elders, these same elders are apt to have leading priestly roles in their respective lineage's ancestor cult, no one of which has greater scope and power than the others. The cult of nonancestral gods exist but are not of great importance for the Ibo. However, in a system where governing authority is more concentrated in the chief, as among the Yoruba, the chief himself is a uniquely important religious figure, performing ceremonies on behalf of the whole tribe as a high priest and becoming himself an object of religious homage.[29] The person of the chief is sacred, and in former times he was kept almost entirely secluded in his palace, either hidden from his visitors by a screen or keeping his face partly covered by a long beaded fringe suspended from his crown. His subjects must prostrate themselves in his presence.

Benin also has a tradition of sacred kinship, and roughly comparable traditions occur in the Igala near the Niger-Benue Confluence, in the Jukun kingdom of the Middle Benue-Valley, and in other small or medium-sized social systems farther north and north-east. Sacred kinship or chieftancy with pagan ceremonies survived alongside Islam until recent times in important northern states; it was suppressed in Bornu only in the mid-nineteenth century and still lingers in the Islamized Nupe Kingdom.

Islam and Christianity, the new faiths, have both been linked with the prestige of comparatively sophisticated urban societies, advanced political structures and far-ranging commerce. They differ in their approach to pagan religions, however. Islam needs no missionary in the Christian sense, and usually the religious pull for converts has been indistinguishable from the spread of Moslem political power and economic influence.[30] Formerly, conversion from paganism was a by-product of extensive subjugation and enslavement. Christian organizations abroad have sent missionaries, who at times were in conflict with the political and commercial representatives, to conduct direct campaigns for converts and offer educational and humanitarian services.

Nearly all shades of acknowledged Christian leanings are represented among Nigeria's 13.2 million Christians. Christians predominate heavily among English-speaking literates and are drawn mainly from the younger age-levels of ethnic groups near the coast, particularly the Ibo, Ibibio, and Yoruba, who are oriented toward western-style enterprise,[31] including cash-crop farming, and literate careers in urban areas. Often the young, educated Christians are members of families who remain mostly unconverted.

In many areas, especially in Southern Nigeria, nominal Christians constitute three-quarters of the population. The churches have become institutionalized.[32] Yet many of the catechists and priests in the Protestant churches have received only a minimum of education—perhaps two years in a theological college after primary school for a catechist; four years for a priest. These men are not, by contemporary standards, highly educated. Little or no study has been made of the doctrines actually preached from their village pulpits, and so they are likely to be much closer to local beliefs and values than to the official doctrines of the churches. Monogamy is expected of communicant members of the churches but not of the mass of the congregations. Church associations are often based upon locally recognized status divisions.[33]The sexes may be separated at Sunday services, while the chiefs may sit in the front pews and be allowed to retain their headgear. In some parts of the country Chiefs and Christians have tacitly compromised on modified rituals so as to enable the latter to achieve those political offices for which their qualifications—age, wealth, and influence make them the more suitable candidates.[34]

Where the southward spread of Islam meets and overlaps with the spread of Christianity, mainly among the Yoruba in the Southwest, Islam tends to excel in the competition for converts, because its immediate demands for readjustment of living patterns are less strict and particularly because Islam does not require the pagan believer to abandon his traditional polygamy. Although conversions of Christians to Islam are more numerous than the reverse, the religious tolerance characteristic of the Nigerian works against intensive efforts to win followers from one another. The missionary efforts of both are concentrated rather on gaining adherents from the pagan groups. Among the Yoruba where Islam is gaining some ground, the Moslem law has not, however, ousted the Yoruba customary law in any sphere, least of all in marriage and land holding.[35] Though Islam has always appeared more tolerant of indigenous social structure, at the present time, its adherents appear more strongly opposed to participation in traditional ritual or secret associations than do most Christians.

On the whole, the primary evangelizing role of missions has been overshadowed by the broader role of their schools, which by providing an introduction to general Western culture open up a new, wider social outlook and equip Nigerians for new career opportunities.[36] They are mainly responsible for the growth of literacy. Missionaries introduced the Western script and provided Bible translation and other religious texts as the earliest publications in previously unwritten languages, such as Yoruba. They founded the earliest schools, developed and conducted almost the entire school system as it developed throughout the Southern half of Nigeria, and established pioneer medical and other welfare services.

Missionary influence has been felt in varied aspects of culture, including such changes as the suppression of twin-killing, among the Ibo, the adoption of Western clothing in place of traditional styles of dress, and the partial absence of polygamy.[37] Some of the changes for which missionaries are mainly responsible have been limited to their Christian converts, but others, more humanitarian than strictly religious in character, have affected much larger numbers. Their total impact in shaping modern Nigerian trends has been tremendous.

Religion has also a political significance throughout Nigeria since traditional governing authority has a religious foundation. The rulers in pagan societies have been pagan chiefs, secret societies, and priestly elders, all embodying and using authority from the unseen world of gods and ancestor-spirits. The native law and custom enforced by them, with regard to marriage and land rights for instance, are thought of as originating from sanctified ancestors and gods whom it would be sacrilege to disobey, risking a dangerous curse as well as penalties by the direct physical force still sometimes commanded by these traditional rulers.

In the Moslem North, pagan law and rulership have been suppressed and supplanted by Islamic institutions which give an alternative form of expression to the underlying general tradition that religious piety and government must be somewhat linked together.[38] Law is based on the Koran, and no sharp distinction is possible between jurisprudence and theology. Emirs claim homage and obedience because of their venerated lines of descent from Moslem holy men, exemplars of piety and militancy against the less orthodox.[39] The most powerful dynasty, formal overlord and model for most others, is that of Sokoto, whose rulers are invested with the holiness of their founding ancestor, Usuman dan Fodio, who established their title, "King of the Moslems," or "Commander of the Faithful" and whose tomb is a shrine of pilgrimage for the pious.[40]

For the purpose of clarity it may be wise to ask why the Sokoto dynasty became the most powerful. The aim of the Emirs (rulers) of Sokoto had been to restore purity to the Islam practiced in the neighboring Hausa Kingdoms. Although they had started by preaching, it became clear that the rulers of Gobir were not prepared to reform, and that Moslems had to be ready to defend themselves and conquer. The nature of the community was scholastic. Though the majority of the scholars were Fulani, many of whom were related to the Emir, the community also included non-Fulani scholars and enjoyed popular support among the non-Fulani population, who doubtless welcomed the Emir's demands for Islamic legality.

When war was declared, however, the community, hitherto primarily scholastic, required military support: this tended to come from the Fulani whose clan-leaders were associated with the community. When the demands of war and of food involved attacking non-Fulani villages, the community lost most of the support among the peasants. Movements in the Jihād[41] were dictated by the need for food and opposition of strong Fulani leaders who could afford the community both food and protection: for wherever the immigrant community stayed, it made enemies of the peasants who had previously been its allies.[42]

With the war, the nature of the community changed. Although the leaders, the family of the Emir, were still dominant, clan-leaders such as Ali Jedo in Sokoto and Namoda in Zamfara superseded in importance the scholars such as the non-Fulani 'Abd-al-Salām. Territorially, the Fulani received the larger share of the land, while the scholars tended to stay by the Emir and "Abdullāh", and the younger men of the community with Bello. The Emir, in conformity with the ideals expressed in his books on Islamic Law and practice, created an elementary administration. Though books were written for their guidance, the men who became territorial leaders seldom had the training suitable for creating an ideal Islamic state. Dissatisfaction with the territorial administration was expressed by the leaders of the community, most forcibly by "Abdullāh." At the death of the Emir, a revolt within Sokoto centered round the non-Fulani scholar 'Abd-al-Salām, while on the borders the Hausa people renewed their hostility to the caliphate. The revolt of 'Abd-al-Salām, aimed in particular at the monopoly of leadership within Sokoto by the family of the Emir but receiving general support from the Hausa under the caliphate, accentuated the need for an organized administration through which Bello could both combat the enemies of the Sokoto caliphate and contain his Fulani supporters, thereby ensuring the continuity of the Emir's community.

The policies of Sokoto toward its immediate neighbors fall into two phases. The first phase, 1827 to C. 1853, was one of conquest in Adar, Gobir, Zamfara and Kebbi. By 1836, after more than forty-seven campaigns Bello had forced the Kebbawa and Zamfarawa into peace, and had driven the Gobirawa and Tuareg out of the area immediately north of the Rima Valley. To close the frontiers, Bello stationed his sons, relatives or companions in ribāts in potentially hostile territory, while nearer to Sokoto were settled immigrant Muslims, often Fulani from outlying areas. Non-Muslim groups who submitted to Sokoto were recognized as protected peoples.

This policy was maintained for some ten years after Bello's death in 1837; it was terminated by a revolt that spread through Kebbi, Burmi and Zamfara and was abetted by the successful leader of the Gobirawa, Mayaki. It proved impossible for Sokoto to put down the revolt completely; instead the ribāts that had been sacked were abandoned.[43]

In the second phase, from C. 1853 to 1903, the policy was largely defensive. The major ribāts were retained, but the new posts in Gobir and upper Zamfara were put under either locally born or locally established leaders. While in Burmi and the upper Sokoto river valley the local rulers were recognized. A treaty, C. 1866, was made in Kebbi; Gobir, with Mayaki dead, was less menacing, with the result that the Sokoto expeditions tended to be punitive, to exact payment and submission. The phase was one of consolidation and increased settlement, which was sufficiently effective so that when a Zamfara revolt occurred in 1891, loyal forces could be mobilized from all sides and the rebels quickly contained.[44]

The military success of Sokoto was inevitable so long as the cohesion of the caliphate was maintained and its enemies lacked co-ordination. As Sokoto fought on interior lines, Kebbi, Zamfara or Gobir could be attacked separately. But they also lacked the unity which Islamic ideals gave to the Sokoto caliphate.

Respect for the Law and Islam was, therefore, the source of authority for the Sokoto caliphate. So long as the caliphate upheld the

Sharia (Islamic Law), he was unimpeachable, and those who denied his authority were unbelievers. Although men might grow less enthusiastic for the Jihād, they did not cease to recognize the Islamic tradition on which it was based: the universal nature of the Law, having an existence and validity separate from Sokoto as established under it. Thus the armies of the subordinate Emirs could be relied upon to fight the wars of Sokoto against anyone who could justly be called a rebel. Clearly, it was in the interests of the subordinate Emirs to maintain the *status quo:* it gave to their position the same universal loyalty which the caliphate possessed. This historical account gives relevance to the Sokoto emirate as the most powerful dynasty, formal overlord and model for most others.

At this point of departure, it may be right to ask what are the current religious practices and trends. Some pagan beliefs and observances persist throughout Nigeria and seem likely to continue for a long time; others are disappearing. Some are modified to compromise with Moslem and Christian requirements, and, conversely, certain Moslem and Christian features are apt to be given a selective emphasis to express a corresponding emphasis in the indigenous religious system. An example is the strongly marked fondness among Yoruba and other southern Christians for memorial services for their deceased relatives. Tendencies to blend indigenous religious traits into Christianity are slightly stronger and more obvious in the independent sects.

As the indigenous faiths are being submerged by conversion to Islam and Christianity, many traditional religious features, such as masked dances and processions representing the dead, are either abandoned or survive as entertainments. Their function shifts gradually in most places, as the unconverted or partly converted continue to regard them in the old way, while more thoroughly Christianized or Islamized members of the community regard them with a varying mixture of hostility and amusement. The hostility is explicitly justified in terms of their adopted religious ban against idolatry, which some take very earnestly.

The Islamic culture of the Northern emirates reflected until recently the conservative piety of their rulers, and the judges they appointed during the 1950's. However, it has become somewhat more receptive to changes paralleling those in other less isolated Moslem countries. With the Nigerian independence, the Emirs have grown more concerned that their own areas reduce their lag in literacy and overall Western-style technical competence in comparison with the non-Moslem areas. The great Islamic synthesis of religion, law, and the social order is beginning to break down. Education is being expanded with new provisions for secular curricula in addition to the traditional Arabic and Islamic studies. Women have also been provided with educational opportunities, though conservative opposition remains strong.

Nevertheless, it is just to say that before the war there existed in Nigeria a much more relaxed relationship between Islam and Christianity than is common in most places where the two religious communities confront each other.

On the whole, the evangelizing of Nigeria involves the degradation of the traditional religious foundations and the establishment of serious inconsistencies (the most notable of which is the impossibility of being at the same time Christian and polygamous). It also involves what has been called by some the expansion of "imported differences," such as those which arise between Christians and pagans or between Christians of different denominations. Thus an African essayist of Central Africa, J. R. Ayoune, harshly blamed the religious confusion on the colonizer and goes so far as to demand that the latter intervene to re-create the lost unity. He condemns "a state of affairs which only has the effect of creating a lamentable confusion in moral development" and adds: "The African, whoever he may be, has a rudiment of religion; to take it away from him and substitute atheism or a confusion of imported religious doctrines is a sure way to make of him an alienated person; he must choose one of them and it is up to the colonizer to find it." [45] "The imported differences" have become a subject of discussion among the African elite group and the African intellectuals. Of imported religions, Leopold Senghor writes:

> Islam and Christianity gave us spiritual values as substitutes (for Negro animism): more elaborate religions; more rational or, to repeat, more attuned to the present age. Once we have chosen them, it's our own task to adapt these religions to our historical and sociological conditions. It is our task to Negrophy them.[46]

But the African can give as well as receive. To this assumption he adds:

The problem which now faces us, Negroes of 1959, is to know how we can integrate Negro-African values into the world of 1959. There is no question of reviving the past, of living in a Negro-African museum; the question is to inspire this world here and now with the values of our past.[47]

Family Structure and Functions

Changes in family structure are closely correlated with the processes of modernization and industrialization. Sociologists, indeed, often argue that the nuclear family is a necessary concomitant of industrial society. But the example of Japan shows that a country may become industrialized and yet retain strong family groupings. It is difficult to assess the type of family structure that Nigeria needs at the present time. Yet we cannot ignore the fact that there are changes going on in the family structure. As men and women move into the modern towns, their relationships with their descent groups are inevitably weakened to some degree, in what manner and to what degree, we shall discuss later on. The reality of the changing social structure is reflected in the persistent arguments— is the extended family a handicap to development? This question is yet to be discussed.

However, among the diverse social traditions in Nigeria, a number of common family relationship patterns emerge, such as respect for age, the high value set on having children, the sharply separate roles for the sexes, bride wealth payments, and polygamy.[48] Most traditions stress descent through the male line. In non-Moslem areas, the male links, reckoned through many generations, serve to join cousins into extensive corporate lineages which are the basic traditional sources for an individual social identity. The Northern Moslem societies differ mainly through their adoption in varying degrees of Islamic family principles, reducing the importance of lineages, increasing the accent on male dominance, and establishing the ideal of female seclusion.[49]

Ties, obligations, rights, and distinctions defined in terms of kinship carry great weight in traditional Nigerian societies. Groups which are bound by common ancestry form the principal or exclusive basis for the organization of social life, land tenure, political roles, and even religion in many of the local traditions. The compact household of one male family head with his wife or wives and their young children may be an important practical unit in its own right, but typically it is regarded as a minor, subordinate part of the much more extensive lineage group founded on descent through the male line from an ancestor several generations back. Kin ties have the greatest relative range and significance in small societies of the Eastern Middle Belt and part of the Southeast, where non-kinship institutions are weak and the range of effective social coordination is about the same as the range of lineage loyalties. In the Moslem North, where land tenure, religion, and civic relationships are not systematically organized on kinship lines, extended lineage ties are not maintained except among the aristocracy, whose privileged status does not rest entirely on genealogy.[50]

Lifelong celibacy is extremely rare for either sex, but the age at first marriage is almost always older for males than for females. Girls usually marry very soon after puberty, young men usually in their twenties. As a man's prosperity increases, it is normal for him to expand his household by additional marriages; the majority of middle-age Nigerian males have two or more wives, though a lot of the Christians do not have more than one wife.[51]

Marriage is regarded primarily as a means of begetting children. Fertility is a paramount value; sterility is dreaded and may be used as grounds for divorce. Although marriages are more or less stable, yet the husband-wife tie is usually much weaker than the tie between either parent and the offspring. First marriages are in principle arranged by the senior kin on both sides.

Three forms of marriages coexist in Nigeria. Indigenous marriage customs permitting unlimited polygamy and based on payment of bride price to the parents of the bride are most common among the non-Moslems as well as Christians. Moslem marriage custom limiting polygamy to four wives is predominant in the North. Christian marriages are not common except among the educated, urbanized Christian elements mainly in the South. The government established a marriage ordinance based on English common law under which a couple may solemnize their marriage before a Christian minister or civil registrar, and which then requires them to observe Christian marriage customs. Marriages under these ordinances are not common because of the restriction it places on plural marriage and easy divorce. They are becoming more frequent, however, particularly among the prominent and growing section of literate city dwellers in the south, who are gradually adopting new attitudes toward marriage and the family in consequence of their education, Christian orientation, and new economic position.[52]

The generic underlying African family patterns remains strongest in all the rural areas of the southern two-thirds of the country, where Islamic influence is lacking or relatively very shallow, as among the Yoruba.[53] Patterns of living for women are kept clearly distinct from those for men, but women are not secluded and in fact often play a vigorous public role. Whenever there is a traditional network of markets for local trading, women conduct all or almost all the trading in most commodities and manage their own discipline with regard to prices and marketing ethics. Since trading is a strongly emphasized part of the adult female role in the South, the sexual division of labor contrasts with the Moslem North, where buying and selling in the market is only a male activity.[54]

Men always have formal dominance in domestic affairs, linked in most systems to an exclusive emphasis on descent through the male line, incorporating children into their father's lineage. However, in a few coastal areas, and in spots along the Eastern flank of the country, matrilineal kinship reckoning persists alongside of, or instead of, the usual patrilineal reckoning. Among the Ijaw in the Niger Delta, children are affiliated with their mother's kin in all cases where only the usual small bride wealth payment has been made. A separate and a less common form of Ijaw marriage with higher payment is required to transfer rights over children to the father and his kin. Among Southeastern groups of the Cross River area, including some Ibo communities, an individual is affiliated both to an extensive male lineage and a comparably extensive female lineage, in which he inherits a separate set of claims and obligations. With regard to any purpose for which descent lines are reckoned through females, children come under the formal authority of their mother's eldest brother and other male heads of the maternal group.[55]

What is the impact of industrialization and of European civilization on the African family which is deemed very important in the entire organization of African life? The importance of the family has been indicated by the large amount of study which has been devoted to the analysis of the effects of European contacts and control in its organization and functioning under changing conditions. In fact the study of the family provides the most fruitful approach to the study of detribalization.[56] Dislocations in any part of the native social structure are reflected in the family, while the disruption of the family system affects the entire social structure. In a comprehensive survey of African marriage and family life it is pointed out that "The family is the most significant feature of African Society," and the family is described as a "central institution."[57] In this study the nature of marriage and the family in African society is described as follows:

> The family itself, in Africa (here Nigeria) as in other parts of the world where people get their subsistence from direct production through the cooperation of kinsmen, is often differently constituted from the grouping to which the name is given in Western society—the unit consisting of two parents with their children which some anthropologists call the elementary family. The feature of African marriage which is perhaps most widely known to the general public is that of polygamy—the legal marriage of one man to two or more women concurrently is permitted. In fact this rule is only one aspect of a system where cooperation in tilling the fields and herding the cattle is provided by a group of people bound by the obligations of kinship and marriage and not by the relationship of wage earner to employer. The larger the cooperating groups the greater the possibilities of wealth and of defense against enemies, and the more children are born to any group, the greater its hopes of expansion in the future. Legitimate children are secured by marriage in due form, and the importance of securing legitimate descendants form the most characteristic features of African marriage law. Women have their own share, an important one, in the division of labor, and both the wealth of the group and its hopes of progeny are greater in proportion to the number of wives.[58]

This description makes it understandable why it is in the family that the disintegration of African society resulting from European contact is most apparent. The disintegration of the traditional family is shown first in the diminishing importance of the collective or group aspect of marriage.[59] Marriage is becoming an arrangement between individuals in which the prospective husband, instead of his kinsmen, provides the bride price, which is so important in cementing family groups. Thus the weakening of the authority of the kinsmen results in the decay of the bonds which used to hold the traditional society together.

In the rural areas the economic factor is largely responsible for the emergence of individual needs and wishes in opposition to the traditional solidarity of kinsmen because of the need for money to pay taxes. Generally the only way that money can be obtained to pay taxes is to seek work in the industrial establishments of foreign investors. The introduction of money into the economy has tended further to secularize the customary bride wealth and weaken the sacred bonds of kinship and the obligations associated with it.[60] As the men become wage-earners, they want to pay the bride wealth in cash rather than in cattle. Where the young men owe their father-in-law certain customary services, they are offering goods and money in the place of these services.

The economic and social factors which have been responsible for the destruction of the traditional Nigerian family in the rural areas become even more destructive in the urban areas. It might be said that the new social forms which are coming into existence are due to urbanization or a new way of life.[61] In the mobile life of the city, where contracts tend to be impersonal, the traditions respecting marriage not only become unsuited to the new social environment but may become an obstacle to marriage. For, as the urbanized native often maintains contacts with the rural natives and may secure a wife from among them conflicts are likely to arise. Sometimes there are conflicts between the girl's parents and the prospective husband over the bride price, which the completely detribalized native may reject on principle.[62] Moreover, since the urbanized native population is drawn from many different tribes, there is no agreement in regard to marriage customs. Conflicts often arise in inter-tribal marriages because of cultural differences, as, for example, the differences in the laws of patrilineal and matrilineal tribes respecting inheritance.

In the urban environment the traditional definitions of the roles of husband and wife in marital and familial relations lose their force, and there is much confusion concerning the responsibilities and duties of the partners in marriage. They find difficulty in adapting their traditional values to those which they recently acquired through their western education, through the cinema and magazines, through their observation (which frequently is misinterpretation) of patterns of behavior in European homes. Once formulated, the expectations of the educated men and women differ from those of their parents. Moreover, although husband and wife may have received an equal measure of western education and broadly profess the same values, their respective marriage roles may well differ, producing strains which can lead to divorce. Modern situations may exacerbate conflicts common in traditional society— such as the rivalry between half brothers, or the desire of the Yoruba wife to become economically more independent of her husband, which runs counter to his needs for her services. Any attempt to establish a polygamous family in the city is rendered impossible because of the character of housing in the city. Then, too, polygamy is generally not countenanced by the municipal authorities if a husband brings a second wife into the house. Among some African tribes it is customary for the wife to cook and work for her mother-in-law before establishing her own house.[63] This means that the native wife in the city must leave her husband and return to his mother in the village.

Similar problems arise in regard to the relations of children with their parents. In the cities, the parents are unable to exercise the same supervision and enforce the same discipline as in rural areas. In the village, the father arranged the marriages of his sons, and his authority could be enforced because he provided his sons with the bride wealth. On the other hand, in the city, where the son is able through his own labor to secure his bride wealth, he may not accept his father's choice of a mate and may insist upon marrying the woman whom he selects. In fact, the city provides many opportunities for young men and women to meet and choose their marriage partners.

As regards the home, it is being replaced by the factory as a unit of production because of the industrialization process. One after another the economic functions of the urban family have been taken over by outside establishments. The transition to a cash crop economy and greater use of imported consumer goods have altered the character of many rural households, since the family work force is partly allotted to tasks for which traditional precedents are lacking. Land tenure is increasingly transferred to an individual basis, subject to cash sale or leasing, and pecuniary considerations have become increasingly dominant in diverse ways. Parents are now primarily concerned for financial profit from their daughters' marriages. However, the most impressive single change which has occurred in family life is the newly independent and aggressive role of youth seen frequently in the south. It is coupled with decline of age, and occasional intergeneration conflict because of the achievement motive that now determines status. Formal deference is still given to the elders in their presence, but their advice or commands do not carry the automatic authority they previously had. The young are too often out of reach, living their own lives according to their initiative and becoming involved in associations which have nothing to do with kinship, such as employment with commercial firms.

The extensive corporate lineages have been losing importance for the same reasons which undermine parental authority. Young people need no longer feel completely dependent on status in the extended kinship group unless they live as farmers on the land, and even then the lineage structure no longer provides in so many places as it once did, the exclusive framework of land tenure on local political rights. Their rights of inherited kinship status are supplemented and at least partly displaced by the more generalized rights of citizenship in the larger political unit and by the impersonal power of money.

Government policy has always been to abstain from direct intervention in family life, except to forbid customs which conflict with contemporary norms, such as twin-killing in the Southeast, marriages of girls under the age of puberty or forced return of wives to their husbands in the Moslem North.[64]

The changes in the structure and functioning of the Nigerian family which have been described thus far are attributable partly to the influence of Christian missionaries and European civilization. Indeed, western civilization has introduced a model family life which contrasts with all the indigenous ones, non-Moslem, and Moslem, in that it is monogamous, stresses the conjugal tie rather than lines of descent, develops greater common ground between masculine and feminine roles (for example, similar education for both sexes), and favors individual freedom, including mutual choice of mates by the young couple themselves. The western family model has been promoted as an ideal by Christian missions and has been adopted to some extent where Christianity is strongest, near the coast.

Social Stratification

The question which arises now is to know in what measure the new social strata foreshadow "classes," in the sense in which they are understood in the industrial societies. One must note, in this connection, that the process of their formation is very different from that which took place in Europe, for example, following the industrial revolution. It is linked to an economic development conditioned by the intervention from the outside (that of a metropolitan power) and gives birth to social categories which, whatever their mutual power relations, are all inferior with respect to the dominant foreign elite.[65] At the initial period the western educated group, which one might call the "economic elite," or economically advanced portion of the population, is usually formed only by means of collaboration with the foreign elite. The Nigerian experience of social stratification is based on the same process.

Nigeria embraces many social systems which were gradually brought closer together under British colonial rule into a new national society. Traditional principles of social structure, which differ from North to South and within each region, remain in force among the great majority (over 80 per cent) of the population and still exert strong influence on urban migrants including the new elite, who usually have close ties with nonliterate, unwesternized relatives outside the town. The structure of traditional societies varied considerably in different parts of the country. Some were relatively egalitarian and democratic (for example, the Ibo society), whereas others stressed rank differences and rule by a permanent aristocracy.[66] In the Northern region, rank contrasts were sharpest in the Northern emirates and most pronounced among the non-Moslem people from the Jos Plateau through the Benue Valley into the Southeast. The coastal people were intermediate, with aristocratic emphasis strongest in the West—and democratic emphasis strongest in the East.[67]

Nearly all the traditional social systems were based on a farming economy, the exception being the Fulani in the North and a few riverine or coastal fishing groups such as the Ijaw in the Niger Delta. For the Northern Moslem societies, the farming population descent of conquered free-men or of imported slaves, was economically and politically subject to a town-dwelling aristocracy, controlling the peasantry through its rural agents.[68] Elsewhere in Nigeria where there was no such distinct aristocracy, society was made up of kinship units which held land inalienably and worked in their own right. Craftsmen and other specialists were usually farmers as well. The chiefs or members of ruling councils represented the competent kinship groups of the whole free population.

Up to the twentieth century, the main type of hereditary ranking found in nearly all the traditional societies was that between free and slave. People were commonly kidnapped and taken as slaves into another society or degraded by their own people and sold away into slavery as penalty for debt or serious breach of custom. The contract of civil rights, work obligations, and style of living between free and slave was not always severe, and slaves might even be adopted as kinsmen by their masters. However, in most places the possible assimilation of slaves into free lineages was gradual over successive generations, and some permanent stigma was apt to remain attached to known slave descent. Enslavement was the main basis for population involvement between different ethnic areas or from any one independent organized local social system to another. Free status with civic rights in one's community of residence was usually dependent on having been born there as an unquestioned descendant from its founder or founders through one of its free lineages.[69]

Everywhere the social rank of individuals was strongly affected by age. Older men generally took precedence and held power over their juniors with whom the slaves were sometimes classed symbolically together as children and youth. Some societies had a formal series of male age-grade organizations, ranked from oldest down to youngest.[70] Age-grade had distinctive functions, the younger children could be assigned collectively to fight in defense of the community or to perform public works such as cleaning the market place. Where male age-grading was most emphasized, there were sometimes female age-grades in a parallel series.[71]

But, a thoroughly distinct social stratum above all the indigenous structures was forced with the advent of the Europeans. Government officials, business representatives and technicians, and missionaries were the three subdivisions of this stratum, which to some extent kept apart from one another and had different types of relations with Nigerians. Officials and businessmen were both ranked in many levels of responsibility, standard of living, and prestige, but even the most modest ranks were looked up to by Nigerians as possessors of the general prestige and exclusive prestige of Europeans. Missionaries usually lived and worked in much closer contact with Nigerians and stayed in the country for longer periods than did persons from the other two categories. The European living quarters, clubs, and other amenities were grouped in separate enclaves called "European quarters." Nigerians were excluded from them, except for rare individuals, until after World War II, when the color bar was officially dropped with regard to both living arrangements and career advancement. In the late 1940's the previously exclusive European stratum became increasingly mixed, with the advancement and inclusion of Nigerians. The behavior and status symbols of the Europeans had been largely adopted as their own by the Nigerians moving to this level.[72]

With this set-up the new indigenous elite arose. The members of this class comprised the English-speaking Africans who were directly subordinate to Europeans in building the new colonial structure in Nigeria. These were from older colonies, (especially Sierra Leone and Ghana), with the later addition of Lagosians and other Southern Nigerians, who gradually supplemented them and came to predominate as clerks, policemen, schoolteachers, and other minor or intermediate-level personnel where literacy and other skills were required. This older nucleus of Western-trained people was greatly expanded by the ever greater numbers of graduates of missions and by the return, after World War II, of those who had gained higher education overseas.[73] The more numerous younger elements showed themselves increasingly ambitious and competitive. Their nationalist leaders and spokesmen sought more aggressively to open up the paths for their advancement in government careers, which was linked to the collective goal of self-government and independence for Nigeria. They aimed at replacing Europeans or moving up into comparative levels throughout the senior service, as well as gaining the prestige, political power, and incomes which would attach to elective parliamentary and ministerial office. Nationalist political pressures also accelerated prospects of advancement to higher responsible levels in the large foreign business firms and hastening over of local control in churches and missions. Politics and civil service careers were decidedly the main avenues for upward mobility, which they exploited, as the former barriers were lowered and their educational qualification rose.

With the arrival of the new elite societal norms have changed drastically. Rewards, sanctions and employment opportunity which were based on ascription are now based on achievement or merit.[74] Social class is no more determined by age and lineage, but by education, occupation and wealth[75]—criteria which modern society uses in judging class. There seems, therefore, to be a transition from the traditional to the open modern society. Hugh Smythe, writing on this transition, stated:

> The tremendous urge and ambition to rise in the social sphere has itself become a major stimulus to getting an education. Making something of oneself is more productive of status than being born into a family of standing in the community; thus ambition is revered above antecedents, valuable though these still are.[76]

This social environment is congenial to industrialization. Nevertheless, in the rural communities, people still refer to the traditional criteria of judging social class. At community meetings they still give preference to people from the old families and descendants of slaves are still being discriminated against, though in a mild form.

On the attainment of independence, political authority shifted from the Europeans to the Nigerians themselves. This resulted in a shift in the leadership struggle from between Europeans and the new elite to the traditional leaders and the new elite. To ingratiate themselves to the masses and to win the support of their rivals (traditional leaders), the new elite looked for an ideology which would provide them with an identity and which would provide a compromise between them and the traditional rulers. This compromise was achieved by the reiteration of certain traditional values and symbols on their accession to power.

Also, as it is the aim of the government (the new elite, owners of authority) to mobilize the entire population in the task of modernization, and to control associations directed to this end, the ideology of the elite is fashioned as a mass religion or Socialism, African Socialism. The political philosophy of the leaders, espoused by a militant party organization, becomes a cause with which the entire population may identify itself. The whole of social life is politicized. We have, however, noted that the African concept of Socialism differs from its western connotation. To the African it means: "A scientific approach to human problems; and it is also identified with planning and specific codes of action." [77] Educated Nigerians hope that they may be able to modernize their society without causing the human suffering that characterized the growth of towns in modern western Europe or the compulsion associated with the development of the U.S.S.R. Again, the stress on the Africanness of their socialism safeguards the Nigerian intellectuals against criticism that it falls short of the connotation it has in the West.

Moreover, the traditional rulers are pacified by the elite by being invited to share in the leadership. This is done by the establishment of the house of chiefs in each of the regions or states, even though most chiefs can neither write nor read. With such political benefits and incentives given to them, the chiefs pledge support to the elite class. The traditional rulers still feel that they are exercising their authority on their communities, though this time by delegating authority to the new elite because they themselves are ignorant of the administrative mechanisms involved in bureaucracy. With this maneuvering, the elite enlist their cooperation and that of the masses who still look up to the chiefs for protection. In turn, the chiefs get a psychological satisfaction by thinking that their authority is not yet obsolete.

The new elite still have another problem, the pacification of the young graduates, school-teachers and technicians. These are not only militant, but also make extravagant demands. They feel the society owes them something.

Commenting on the elite-traditional leaders rivalry and the elite-masses relationship, Sir Henry Willink wrote:

> The relationship between the new elected government and the traditional forces represented by chiefs is one that confronts every government in Nigeria and has a certain superficial resemblance to the problems which in England faced the Tudor kings when they attempted to establish a central monarchy after the chaos of the wars of the Roses.[78]

Considering these relationships between the classes, what then are the new lines of stratification? In Nigeria, the relative fluidity of class alignments, the short period over which the "new" elite class has developed, and the relatively small emphasis upon lineage in the new elite, all combine to make the line between class levels difficult to draw. Nevertheless, we can stratify the new society thus:

Western-Educated Elite	Politicians, old graduates
Traditional Rulers	Chiefs
White Collar	Young graduates, technicians, estate workers
Unskilled Laborers	Subsistence farmers, laborers
Unemployed	Subsistence—dependents on relations[79]

The new elite based primarily on Western education has, therefore, permeated political and professional hierarchies and is rapidly moving to those high-ranking positions in the economy formerly more tightly held by Europeans rather than to leading positions in other sectors of the society. The group is more conscious of its distinction from the uneducated (from which it has sprung) than of the ethnic diversity within it. It tends to cut across the ethnic lines and thus constitutes the most national—and hence for the future—most significant group in Nigerian society. Relatively few members of this elite are conscious of their responsibility to lead their uneducated compatriots into the modern world. Most are preoccupied with solidifying their own position and in gaining the prerequisites of membership to an elite class—large houses, automobiles, radio and television sets, European-style clothing, membership to elite clubs.

In the rural areas, and more especially in the Northern Region, where the traditional rulers retain much of their power and prestige, the new elite has not yet gained a secure leadership position. Most of these traditional rulers, however, have either joined the educated class or are training their children to belong to the new elite. Within a space of little over a single generation the balance of power and prestige has, even outside the urban areas of the South, shifted decisively toward the new elite, and the indications are that the transfer will be virtually complete within the next generation.

In concluding the chapter, one needs to note the distinctive sets of social values which characterize the various ethnic groups. In the far North, the major ethnic traditions are strongly influenced by the comprehensive value system of Islam and centuries of experience with far-reaching political and commercial relationships. This permanence of traditional and religious experience makes the North resist Westernization and modernization. As a result, the North is still very traditional—a situation which creates a developmental gap between the North and the South. Near the coast, new values have been introduced by contacts with Western civilization; there is much overlapping or a certain compromise in the transition from old to new standards. Since the coast is more receptive to change, the process of differentiation, adaptation and integration as well as industrialization are more rigorous there. Most of the industries are in the South because of the ready availability of local labor and their zeal to learn new techniques and adapt to the new way of living—urban life, a concomitant of industrialization.

Also, European contact has brought about a "makeshift" process in the traditional institutions like the family which is drifting toward the nuclear type. The social stratification has assumed new lines, breaking through the traditional structure, and these changes have resulted in individualism, unknown to the native population and new kinds of secondary associations, for example, economic and educational associations. So it seems as if the society is following what Harbison and his co-authors called the "logic of industrialization." [80]

The above conclusions had some relevance before the civil war because of the tribal differences in achievement and motivation to modernize. Now many Nigerian and African scholars are beginning to question the validity of the stereotypes credited to the Ibo by the Africanists. Examples of these stereotypes are their receptivity to change and high achievement motivation, their aggressive competition and their willingness to explore new avenues of power and status, their non-hierarchical social structure and their noncompliance to formal authority. Levine in a study of Nigerian male secondary school students reported his findings thus:[81]

1. The frequency of achievement imagery in dream reports was greatest for the Ibo, followed by the Southern Yoruba, Northern Yoruba, and Hausa, in that order, as predicted by the status mobility hypothesis. The Ibo-Hausa and Southern Yoruba-Hausa are statistically significant. The order of the groups does not correspond to their ranking on frequency of educated parents. Differences of groups comprised on the basis of mothers' education are extremely small in the sample as a whole and in the Ibo and Yoruba subsamples. Moslem-Christian differences are highly significant but almost entirely confounded with ethnic group membership. Among the Northern Yoruba, the only group with enough adherents of both religions, there is no difference in frequency between Moslems and Christians.

2. The frequency of obedience and social compliance value themes in essays on success written by the students was greatest for the Hausa, followed by the Southern Yoruba and Ibo, in that order. The Ibo-Hausa and Yoruba-Hausa differences are statistically significant.

In a nation-wide public opinion survey of Nigerian adults, Levine's report was as follows:

1. The proposition of persons mentioning self-development or improvement as a leading personal aspiration was greatest for the Ibo, followed by the Southern Yoruba and Fulani-Hausa, in that order. Ibo-Fulani-Hausa and Southern Yoruba-Fulani-Hausa differences were highly significant statistically.

2. The proportion of persons mentioning improvement of standard of living or national prosperity through technological advance as a leading aspiration for Nigeria was greatest for the Ibo, followed by the Southern Yoruba and Fulani-Hausa, in that order. Ibo-Fulani-Hausa and Southern Yoruba-Fulani-Hausa differences were highly significant statistically.

Seibel (1967) in his study of "Some Aspects of Inter-Ethnic Relations in Nigeria," came up with similar findings depicting the Ibo as the most ascetic.[82] Findings of this nature raise great criticisms from a lot of African academicians in the field. They question the validity of such studies and often wonder whether the researchers are biased toward proving a-priori prepositions and stereotypes. Do other Nigerian tribes really lack the special qualities which are the dynamic forces of modernization and economic development? How does McClelland's idea of achievement motives fit say other tribes beside the Ibo? The achievement motive concept, according to McClelland, is the drive toward acquisition. The rate of development and modernization of any society depends on a number of highly motivated people within that society. In the Western societies, the entrepreneurs with their high motivation toward achievement set the pace of development and modernization. Similarly the Ibo are considered to be the forerunners of development because they possess great entrepreneurial skills. As we have noted above, there is almost a consensus among African scholars that the validity of such generalizations about the Ibo is questionable and at best it is circumstantial. Circumstantial in that it is (a) a sheer historical accident, (b) a question of geographical and population factors.

Let us first consider the question of "sheer historical accident." The Ibo could certainly be considered to have suffered a *withdrawal of status respect* during the early colonial period. What does *withdrawal of status respect* mean. Hagen[83] has raised the question of why a "traditional society" or some group within it will suddenly abandon traditional ways and turn its "energies to the task of technological advance." His theoretical answer is that "the basic cause of such change is the perception on the part of the members of some social group that their purposes and values in life are not respected by groups in the society whom they respect and whose esteem they value." [84] The group so affected by "withdrawal of status respect" is first demoralized and then prompted to find alternative means of righting itself with the disparaging wider society. In so doing—a process which Hagen believes to involve changes in child rearing and personality development—the group assumes a role as technological and economic inventor thus promoting economic growth in a hitherto stagnant society. Can this concept of withdrawal of status respect account for the differences in achievement gradients among our three Nigerian groups? We must examine their history under colonial administration to find out.

Before British administration the Ibo constituted a relatively isolated cluster of societies although they traded with coastal groups and some of their neighbors. Contrary to the Ibo cluster of societies were the great Kingdoms of Benin, Yoruba and the Northern emirates of Kano, Sokoto, Katsina and Gwando. Kano was a great commercial center trading with the Arabs and the other afore-mentioned Kingdoms. The British found the Islamic emirates in the north intransigent, and so they set up a number of trading points on the Southern coast. British administration was established in 1903 when the submission of Sokoto and Kano was followed by the emirates of Katsina and Gwando accepting British supremacy. The conditions of settlement imposed, included the passing of all rights of conquest from the Fulani to Great Britain; sultans, emirs and principal officers of state holding appointments from the British Government in obedience to the laws of Britain.

In the South, British presence was a matter of slave-trading and exploration until 1861 when possession was taken of Lagos. In 1879 private British trading interests, in the face of the challenge of two French firms supported by the French Government amalgamated to form the United Africa Company.[85] In 1884 the latter bought out the French interests. In 1886 the United Africa Company received a royal charter and became the Royal Niger Company. As a result of the Berlin Conference, the coast lands known as the Oil Rivers became a British Protectorate under the control of the Royal Niger Company. Between that date and 1909, Anglo-French interests were in conflict in the west of the territory. The situation was such that in 1900 the Company surrendered its charter and the territories were designated by the name Nigeria and were placed under the political control of the Crown. Boundary demarcations were agreed with the French in the west and north and with the Germans in the east.

The various parts of the country were almagamated in 1904, but provincial organization continued to follow the tripartite division of the country. The adoption of a policy of indirect rule through the traditional instruments of chiefs also served to emphasize the differences between the Southeast, the Southwest, and the North.

The efflorescence of missionary endeavor coincided with the European, especially the British, interest in the commercial and political drive to penetrate the interior of the country. Whilst the missionary effort was concerned with the redemption and the regeneration of the people of the "Dark Continent," it was also concerned with the material well-being of the people. In consequence, missionaries, traders, and later government agents collaborated in opening up the country.

The initial missionary effort in Western Nigeria was soon followed by enterprises in the Niger Delta and Eastern Nigeria. In the North missionary education activity developed much more slowly and on a smaller scale. This was in part due to the agreement made between the British Government and the emirs following the pacification of the North, when it was agreed that Christian missionaries should not be admitted to the emirates without the consent of the emirs. This resulted in missionary effort being largely confined to the pagan areas apart from the administrative restrictions upon mission educational effort, there was antagonism toward Western education due to the existence of a loose system of Koranic schools. In these schools boys, and occasionally girls, learnt by rote large sections of the Koran, were trained in correct methods of worship and taught the basic laws of social conduct by the local "mallam" or teacher. Apart from the risk that European type of schooling might make the pupils indifferent to faith, there was a general antipathy toward things Western. Their antipathy was confirmed by the fact that Western education was identified with evangelization in the country generally. Victor Murray in his book, *The School in the Bush,* commented:

> To all intents and purposes the school is the church. Right away in the bush or in the forest the two are one, and the village teacher is also the village evangelist. An appreciation of this fact is cardinal in all considerations of African education.[86]

Whilst this identification initiated the development of education in both Southern and Northern Nigeria, in the rest of the country it contributed to the growth of a new social group which provided the leadership for the new nationalism of the twentieth century.

The approach to education produced by the missionaries was based upon the certainty of the Christian message, but it was also based upon the assumption of the superiority of Western civilization and the evil of paganism. African customs, beliefs and practices, family life and even the institution of chiefdom were, with few exceptions, regarded as repugnant. Christianity was confused with Western civilization. The Nigerian was to be remade in the image that the missionaries brought with them. This was the basis of the northern resistance to missionary infiltration. They were civilized and sophisticated in their own way; so also were the Yoruba Kingdoms and the Benin Kingdom. But the latter two yielded because of the British conquest.

What can we deduce from the wide digression into historical data? With the setting up of trading points in the South, there arose a demand for labor, mostly unskilled and clerical labor. It is at this point that we can apply the "withdrawal of status respect" hypothesis. The Hausa-Fulani would not condescend to any type of manual labor under foreign supervision. The Yoruba and the Effik, who had had much more Western contact and education and were firmly entrenched in the higher civil service and professional jobs would not revert to manual labor. The only people left to provide manual labor in the construction industry and other petty service industries were the Ibos. The Ibos were despised by the rest as a people whose traditional culture lacked cloth and clothing, urbanism, and political centralization. Being despised in this way must have hurt many Ibos profoundly. Out of their resentment at being despised as a backward people, and also at being discriminated against in jobs and housing in towns dominated by ethnic groups, may have come the tremendous Ibo determination to get ahead, to be more modern than anyone else, to favor technological advance, and to succeed in every field individually as a group.

It can be argued with equal cogency that the events since 1900 have afforded the Hausa maximal protection from the withdrawal of status respect which often accompanies colonialism. In the system of indirect rule they were allowed to retain their own rulers and continue the traditional life (which was a sort of civilization in itself) fostered by those rulers. Lord Lugard's agreement, as we have noted above, insulated them from Christian missionaries and Western education, so that they never suffered the jolts to cultural self-esteem which are inflicted on a non-Western people by Christianity, knowledge of the outside world, and by a new scale of educational values. In other words, they continue to see as undiminished in splendor their traditional culture with its monarchy, orthodox

Islam, orientation toward Mecca, and Koranic schooling. They did not suffer the invidious comparison with European culture or Europeanized Africans which Southern Nigerians did. Furthermore, they maintained autonomy until they were able to enter into a federation with the southern regions with themselves as the dominant leaders, having a majority of the voting population under their control. Hence, when the Hausa-Fulani political leaders came to Lagos, they came as the rulers of the Federation of Nigeria, but with some qualification. They formed a coalition government with the Ibo who were ambitious for prestige and power. And since the Hausa-Fulani lacked the European sophistication which was requisite for running a democratic government, the Ibo, who had the sophistication, were by and large the political leaders. They made use of their new power adequately by restraining the Yoruba, their chief rivals, from competing with them for positions. (This phenomenon was not exclusive to the Ibos. The Yorubas also did the same thing.) In terms of educated people and commercial or trading spirit, the Hausa-Fulani and the Yoruba have a long tradition of trans-Saharan trade behind them. The Ibo commercial experience is new, but it started at an appropriate time, when the Nigerians were being studied by Africanists, and when the Ibo were in virtual authority. Moreover, their own commercial experience was Western and hence Western scholars in dire necessity to justify Westernization had no option but to heighten the asceticism, individualism, aggressiveness, and the commitment to modernity of the Ibo. The question to ask now is, if they were so achievement motivated, if they were so prone to modernize, why did they have to wait until they were forced by circumstance (the advent of the Europeans) to develop any index of modernity. We know the Yoruba civilization, the Benin civilization and the Hausa-Fulani civilization existed before the advent of the Europeans. It leaves one wondering how valid are the stereotypes attached to the Ibo. Indeed, the Effik, a sub-tribe in the East, were as receptive to change as the Ibo, if not more.[87] But because of the power hypothesis, mentioned above, the Ibo were able (out of their population majority) to restrain the Effiks in their activities and hence put a stop to their modernizing and enterprising spirit.

If, then, we view the three ethnic groups (Ibo, Hausa-Fulani, and Yoruba) in terms of the hypothesis derived from Hagen that withdrawal of status respect leads to something like 'n' achievement, we can indeed find support for such an hypothesis. The Ibo, leading in 'n' achievement, certainly suffered the most complete group loss of respect during the colonial period; the Hausa, lowest on 'n' achievement, were most insulated from the conditions producing social disparagement in a colonial society, and the Yoruba, in a sense, had it both ways. "On the basis of our Nigerian comparison," writes Levine, "we cannot reject the theory which views achievement striving as a reaction to group disparagement, and we admit it as a plausible explanation of our findings." [88] But he raises the question that how can the theory explain the greater achievement orientation of the pre-colonial Ibo as compared with the Hausa and Yoruba. We clarified this doubt, when we asked why the Ibo had no form of civilization before the advent of the European. If they were so achievement oriented, why should they fail to show signs of it either by urbanism of some sort, or by a form of central government or any index of modernity? Why was their backwardness so pronounced and why had they relied on a chance factor, political maneuvers, to prove their achievement orientation?

Another reason we find from analyzing the data on the three tribes for the greatest asceticism among the Ibo is cushioned in the hypothesis of "contemporary status mobility patterns." The basic idea in this hypothesis is that the frequency of 'n' Achievement in a group is determined primarily by the more or less accurate perception of the growing male child as to: the chances of his rising socially, and the behavior which leads to success in the status system. His perception is determined by the information concerning the state of the system which he receives from various individuals and institutions, including older members of the family, school-teachers, religious instructors, books, and mass media. Let us assume that he forms a fairly stable image from these diverse sources of information by the time he is fourteen years old. If his image is that the chances of his rising socially are good and that individual competition with a standard of excellence is what leads to success, then he will manifest the achievement motive. If his image is that he has little chance of rising socially and that obedience and social compliance lead to what success is available, then he will vary between these extremes, according to the amount of the perceived opportunities and the strength of the perception of achievement behavior as instrumental in success. Thus the frequency of 'n' Achievement in a population will co-vary with the strength of the incentives for achievement behavior perceived by the men as being offered by status mobility system during the years in which they were growing up. In this theory there is little time lapse between changes in status mobility system and changes in 'n' Achievement, at least in the younger generation, and neither parental values nor child-training practices are involved as mediating variables—only the transmission of information.

How does this theory apply to the Nigerian situation? Levine in his *Dreams and Deeds in Nigeria,* states that the Hausa-Fulani boys' idea of status mobility is least compared to the Yoruba boys' and the Ibo boys', and the Yoruba boys' notion is less than the Ibo boys'. He writes:

> The conclusion is that our sample of Hausa students, and Fulani-Hausa adults surveyed in the national poll, had their level of achievement motivation formed by a status system which, now as in the past, does not offer strong incentives for independent achieving behavior.[89]

African scholars tend to disagree with this assumption for they contend that the Ibo are as compliant as any other tribe. Morrill likens the Ibo culture to the Chinese because both are made up of separate and more or less autonomous villages. The primary loyalty of the individual is to the village and not to a social or political above the village.[90] Implicit in this statement two inferences could be made. The fact that the individual exhibits some form of compliance, at least to his village, shows that his village exercised some authority over him. And authority implies sanction and rewards. So the Ibo boy was not as free as he has been portrayed to be. Besides, if there is great status mobility among them, why have the Christian missionaries failed to uplift the social status of the *Osu* (a descendant of a slave)? Why is he up to now still being stigmatized and why has his movement in the social scale been stifled? Another inference to be made is that the Ibo owe allegiance to the village chief or head because that was the only form of political organization he knew. As a result when modern political organizations were in vogue, they did not hesitate to rally to them—a sign of compliance to formal authority. A recent example is their complete obedience to Ojukwu, the former Biafran leader. One would think that a people who are supposedly individualistic and who have status mobility patterns would have raised objections to the legitimacy of Ojukwu's authority, especially since every one of them was disgusted with the war. Morrill's comparison of their culture to the Chinese brings out clearly their compliance to formal authority. On the other hand, it is not totally true that the Ibo society was nonstratified. Recent studies are indicating that some of the Ibo societies were classified; for example, the Northeastern Ibos, the Onitsha and the Aros. One could argue that the stratification of the Onitsha Ibo and the Northeastern Ibo was due to the Benin influence on Onitsha and the Tiv influence on the Northeastern Ibo, but the question of the Aros still remains unclarified. They are, indeed, the central Ibos.

Moreover, Levine's findings could be challenged further. The lack of high 'n' Achievement among the Hausa school boys and the Fulani-Hausa adults could have been due to some other variables rather than the question of "contemporary status mobility patterns." We have already mentioned the power hypothesis, that is, who really held the reigns of power in the country even though the Hausa-Fulani were supposedly the political power holders. It was the Ibo who controlled the civil service and commerce. This we have shown was an accident of history because of their forced exposure to Western civilization. That was their only alternative and with time, when modernization became the ideal of all traditional society, they became more advantageous because they had the Western education and they formed the right political alliance. With them in virtual control in the North, it was not an uncommon practice for those of them at the top to create opportunity for their kins at the expense of the other tribes, especially the Hausa-Fulani Western-educated types. If they could not compete in their region, what was the guarantee they would be successful in the Southern regions which were comparatively far more modernized? This was the basis of the Northernization policy by Ahmadu Bello, the then Northern Premier, to create opportunity for the citizens of the North. What conclusions can we draw from this experience? The Levine findings could have been influenced by factors like the ones above where the Ibo at the top were preventing aspirants of other tribes, but promoting their own. The mere fact that the Ibo boy knew that he could get a good position after graduation became an impetus to aspire higher. The converse of this of course also holds true for boys of other ethnic groups. The Hausa-Fulani boy became less motivated not because of his traditional obedience to authority and his contentment with his status, but because he was frustrated with the fear of not getting a respectable position in the society. This throws the validity of the Levine findings into doubt.

Another reason which could explain the high 'n' Achievement among the Ibo besides the reasons of sheer historical accident and the power hypothesis, is the *population pressure* hypothesis. The basic point here is that the Ibo homeland in Eastern Nigeria is one of the most densely populated regions in Africa, and over-population could be responsible for their non-agricultural occupations. With regard to this, Horton stated:

> The Ibo people of Eastern Nigeria have become renowned in recent years for the value they set on aggressive competition, the struggle for achievement, and the willingness to explore new avenues of power and status. A culture and personality theorist, whom I talked to about them, took this value as an obvious 'ultimate,' to be interpreted as the effects of certain causes—possibly in the realm of child-training. As a social anthropologist, I was suspicious of this. I pointed to the fact that over much of the Iboland there is acute land shortage, that anxious parents quite 'reasonably' encourage their children to struggle for a school success that will fit them for some career other than farming, and that when the children grow up, their own 'reason' tells them that their only hope of a comfortable existence lies in continuing the struggle in outside trade, or in jobs in government or the big commercial firms. To back up this interpretation, I pointed to the fact that in pockets of adequate land supply like Nike and Abakiliki, where everyone can still get along comfortably in a farming career, this syndrome of aggressive competition and readiness to exploit new avenues of advancement is not at all obvious.[91]

Horton's hypothesis is that Ibo achievement behavior is a conscious, rational adaptation to an obviously difficult economic situation. The implication is that the Ibo response is that of any rational man in a coercive environment who is reasonable enough to want "a comfortable existence." Some social scientists do not believe this rationalistic view helps explain the most important aspects of the Ibo "syndrome of aggressive competition." The important aspect of Ibo achievement-behavior overlooked by Horton, they claim, is that it was not the only "reasonable" cause of action open to them. When a rural family is faced with a decline in income such as that caused by overcrowding on the land, they argue, there is a choice between lowering standards of consumption and finding new sources of income. The former alternative, which involves becoming accustomed to increasing poverty, is in fact adopted by families in economically depressed areas all over the world. Such families operate on a principle of least effort in which the comfort of remaining in familiar surroundings and doing familiar things, even when faced with starvation, outweighs the future economic benefits that might be gained from drastically changing their way of life. So long as their impoverishment is gradual, they will put up with it, for it affords known and immediate gratifications that would be missing were they to seek new productive activities. Their behavior is by no means totally irrational; it is based on a short-run hedonistic calculus into which long range considerations do not enter. To persons predisposed to adopt this course of action (or inaction), the Ibo willingness to uproot themselves and give up accustomed if reduced rewards, seems unreasonable and unnatural. The reply to this objection is that the Ibo had no option for they had to carry out the menial jobs. There were no Indians around like in East Africa to perform the manual work. The Ibos became the Indians of Nigeria. It was not a question of their choice, but of compulsion.

However, one thing seems certain from all this argument about what tribe has a higher achievement motivation than the others. As we noted above, a lot of African scholars are raising objections as to the characterization of the Ibo as the most enterprising and ascetic. The reasons for their objection I have tried to present in this chapter. If, indeed, the Ibo have the highest 'n' Achievement, it is yet to be more validly proven. The civil war has awakened every tribe to the concepts of modernization and achievement. The former variables which were supposed to have favored one tribe at the expense of others have been removed with the creation of states—the dislocation of the former political machine which gave virtual power to one tribe. Now is the time to really measure the 'n' Achievement of the different tribes. The validity and reliability for such a study would be more sound because some of the mediating variables have partly, if not totally, been controlled or removed. Until such investigations are carried out, we cannot be certain about the relationship of achievement orientation of a tribe to economic achievement.

III
MIGRATION FROM RURAL
COMMUNITIES TO URBAN CENTERS

It may at this stage be expedient to define the two processes of industrialization and urbanization for the purpose of clarification. "Industrialization" represents a particular stage in human knowledge and in man's command over nature—a stage at which man has learnt the arts of machine production and the use of mechanical power on a large scale but has not so much become the master of these new arts as to bring them to full maturity or under fully satisfactory control. It is a phase in material process, but only a phase to be superseded when its development has become sufficiently complete.

Fundamentally it is an affair of productive technique. It is based upon the discovery and exploitation of improved methods of producing wealth, primarily in the processes of manufacture but also to an increasing extent in agriculture and in the extractive industries yielding primary products. It is closely associated with an increase in the scale of production, with the development of capitalistic methods in both manufacture and marketing and with the employment of wage labor. Its secondary effects have included hitherto a concentration of the population in densely inhabited urban areas, a very rapid increase in the much lending of capital for development by the more advanced countries to those less advanced and a very rapid increase in the numbers and social importance of the middle classes, including those engaged in the professions as well as the administration and supervision of industry and commerce.

"Urbanization," on the other hand, is characterized by movements of people from small communities concerned chiefly or solely with agriculture to other communities, generally larger, whose activities are primarily centered in government, trade, manufacture or allied interests. Although there were earlier eras, as for example, in Greece during the age of Pericles and during the Roman Empire, when the movement of people to the city presented serious problems, the phenomenon has become relatively important since the onset of the Industrial Revolution. Urbanization depends to a large extent on the degree to which industrial and mercantile products are divorced from agriculture. In short, it is the process of becoming urban, moving to cities, changing from agriculture to other pursuits common to the cities, and, corresponding changing of behavior patterns.

In studying urbanization in newly or rapidly developing countries, it is important to divest oneself of the Western image of urbanization. This process is absolutely mandatory, though difficult. For example, it is important to imagine a kind of urbanization in which there may be very little transportation, as in the case of a city in India with a population of more than 2,000,000, in which the number of automobile vehicles—cars, trucks, and buses—amounts to only 20,000. This is a very great contrast to the Western urbanization with which we are familiar.

The vast majority of such urban populations in newly developing countries will consist of recent migrants to the city, in contrast to Western cities. Most of these migrants would have no handle on their society, that is, they will have no means to achieve control of their environment in which they are living. This is in complete contrast to Western forms of urbanization where delegative, representative governments have been developed to the point where by means of such representation, as well as by pressure group activities, the ordinary citizen can make some impact on the environment in which he lives. The vast majority of urban populations in newly developing countries has a quite different level of living from that found in urbanized western countries.

Another new concept, "subsistence urbanization," is currently being used in sociological parlance. The familiar concept of subsistence agriculture connotes a level of living derived from agricultural production on which one can barely exist and which therefore permits no surplus to be exported, sold, or otherwise disposed of for funds to improve the standard of living. There is a kind of parallel subsistence in the urbanization, according to Gerald Breese, in his "Urbanization in Newly Developing Countries." This implies the urbanization in which the ordinary citizen has only the bare necessities, and sometimes not even those, for survival in the urban environment. This is not a very complimentary description of urbanization in newly developing or modernizing countries, but the evidence seems to indicate that the vast majority of people in such places does indeed live on a level of subsistence urbanization. The readily observable evidence, in addition to available data of the conditions in which the residents live, consists of their generally very low level of housing, their diet, the clothing that they can afford to buy, and what amenities of life are available to them. This is an urbanization of very high density, of individuals living under conditions that may be even worse than the rural areas from which they have come, of not having available the kinds of work or the means of support which will permit them to do more than merely survive.

Although Anglo-European countries have by no means resolved all of the problems of urbanization in their domains, it nevertheless, appears evident that world-wide urbanization is taking place in a peculiar context; this raises many questions and fails to resolve many issues. David E. Lilienthal said in his "Metropolitan Area Problems" that:

> This is a world-wide phenomenon . . . The impact of urban growth may be even greater in the underdeveloped countries than in the industrialized nations, for it is occurring on top of a mass of other problems which North Americans and Europeans have to some degree already solved: political stability, independence, relative economic stability, decent living standards, and orderly and flexible social structure. This is truly new international frontier of great importance.

Lilienthal's comment calls attention to the many ramifications of the new kind of urbanization being superimposed upon and developing within a different context from the urbanization with which we are already familiar. It is within this different context that we want to consider Nigerian urbanization.

Aside from the migratory seasonal grazing of the "cattle" Fulani in the North, which sometimes oversteps international boundaries, there is seasonal migration of labor between rural and urban areas. Permanent moves to the city are increasing as education spreads and more jobs become available. But, at first, most moves were seasonal or temporary, partly because of the growing attachment to tribe, family, and ancestry and partly because immigrant settlers suffer social and legal disabilities.

For the areas where the farmers grow neither surplus from crops nor an export crop, the main source of cash income is wage labor. But because the processes of production are economically so backward, local employment is scarce, except perhaps where the government decides to construct a major highway. To find work, men travel seasonally, or for periods of two or three years, to the richer regions. Their journeys help to broaden their horizons. They become aware of the affluence of neighboring regions and the comparative poverty of their own. But the man who enjoys the former is more likely to stay in these regions than try to exploit opportunities at home, while it is the less ambitious who save what they can and return to become absorbed in the traditional way of life.

In the colonial era, the above reasons encouraged migration, but these reasons do not explain the migration of today. Many other factors are now involved.

Industrialization and urbanization have resulted in the dislocation of native peoples. The two processes are often closely tied up.[1] In order to mechanize agriculture, there has been an industrialization of agriculture through the development of plantations (as noted in Chapter V) and industrial estates are also increasing in number. In order for these industrial projects to function successfully, adequate labor is necessary. These employment opportunities attract people from all over the country.

The cities themselves are elements of attraction to the rural population. Indeed, most of the migration to the burgeoning Nigerian communities has been from relatively nearby villages and towns. According to the census of 1953, nearly three-fourths of the inhabitants of Lagos were from the contiguous Western Region of Nigeria (However, over a twenty-year period people who had come to Lagos from the Eastern Region increased five times as compared with the doubling of those from the Western Region).[2] Traditional migration routes have been unrelated to European political fortunes, rather they are related to the natural African lines of demarcation.[3] Accordingly, the city has sometimes drawn population from another nation or territory; the addition may be temporary or permanent.

We have seen the economic factor that contributes to migration in search of job opportunities. There are non-economic factors as well. The city offers a means of escape for those whose village life is disagreeable or limited—those who feel unwanted, unsuccessful, in disgrace, or out of favor with local authority or even with sorcerers; those who hunger for more education or new horizons to explore; those who aspire to achievement beyond that possible, in the village. An aged mother may move to the city to live with her urban son; a village girl may marry a city man; a servant may move with his employer.[4]

In a few rural areas the density of population is becoming so great that there is not sufficient land to provide an adequate living; it is from the rural parts of the Ibo country that emigration is heaviest, and so villages report half their adult men absent at any one time. School leavers, unwilling to farm in the manner of their parents, go to town to seek wage employment.[5]

The migrants may be most conveniently classified into three groups: the seasonal, the short-staying, and the long-staying.[6] The seasonal migrants come predominantly from the savanna region, where the long dry season, during which little or no work is needed on the farms, permits the young men to travel vast distances to employment. Annually, a quarter million men from Sokoto Province and neighboring territories travel southward.

Many of the short-staying migrants—men who remain in the town for a year or two before returning to the village, perhaps only for a similar period—are termed "target workers." They come to town to earn sufficient money for a specific purpose, and when they have achieved their aim, they return home. They tend to live poorly in the town, maximizing their savings, and they also usually learn no skills.

Save for the educated youths, there are perhaps few men who arrive in town with the intention of staying permanently. But those who make good in trade or through the acquisition of a skill which guarantees permanent employment and a better wage, will tend to remain in town. The possibilities of gaining a similar income grow less, while their urban affluence, demonstrated by their beneficence on visits home, enhances their prestige in the village. Those, on the other hand, who fail to make good in the town are reluctant to return to their villages penniless; they are more likely to stay on, hoping for better luck, until their kinsmen lose patience with their indigence and forcibly repatriate them.

These patterns of migration raise questions about the stability of a Nigerian city (or nearly all West African cities for the Nigerian experiences hold true for them too). Most men would have resided in them for a short time only, whatever their long-term intentions. Few surveys have been conducted to measure the stability of urban residence and the patterns of migration.[7] It seems probable nonetheless that there is, in West Africa as a whole, a rapidly increasing tendency for men to stay longer in the towns, and to have their wives and children with them. This may partly be explained by the increasing shortage of land in the rural areas or by the increasing immigration to the town of literates. It is probably also due to an increasing proportion of semi-skilled and skilled work in urban employment. In Nigeria, during the past decade, the number of employed persons has increased but slightly, relative to the visible expansion in government services, commerce and manufacturing; many of the activities which formerly absorbed large numbers of unskilled laborers—road building, for instance—are now mechanized.

Rural Life

The household unit is variable in size and structure. In the prevalent rural situation and to a large extent in towns, as in the traditional urban clusters of the Yoruba, it is arranged physically in a compound with a wall or fence enclosing a number of separate small buildings or rooms which open into a common central open space. The male head of the compound and any additional male adults, who may be his younger brothers or grown sons, each have their private quarters, and there are separate quarters for each married woman with her children. Factors increasing the number of persons who live in one compound are polygamy and the variable practice of adult brothers living together, with their respective groups of wives and children. Three, or sometimes even four, generations may be found within a compound. It is not unusual for an elderly widow to live with her eldest son or a group of sons in one place.[8]

On the other hand, contrary to what might be expected, the typical rural dwelling although lacking in comfort, does present some advantages from the angles of hygiene and sturdiness as compared to the dwellings of the workers' sector proper. This is because the rural dwelling is adapted to the world in which the Nigerian peasant lives; it is accessible to him because he himself is in charge of building it, and the materials used are found in the very surroundings of the village.

The growing of export crops has become a major occupation of the rural dwellers. Most cacao farmers rely on seasonal migrant labor or on local men who are themselves farmers but who need immediate cash. This cultivation of export crops has increased the pressure on land to the point where it is barely enough for everybody. The usual initial reaction is to insist that a man farms "where his father did," and requests for land from maternally related groups are received much less favorably than in the past. One is much more dependent upon one's own group, and can less afford to offend his elders. The enhanced cohesion that this produces in the descent group is parallel in the case of urban land. Frequently this gains a high economic value and, among the Yoruba, for instance, is sold. The descent group thus becomes a land management agency, whose profits from transactions are shared among all members. Ultimately, land shortage results in increasing individualizations of land holding; a father's farms are shared among his own sons who are likely to be able to find additional land. Even smaller segments of the descent group acquire the right to alienate land by lease or sale. This process has probably gone furthest among the Ibo of Eastern Nigeria, in whose central districts population densities of over one thousand per square mile are recorded.[9]

> The traditionally-styled compounds (wrote Lloyd) are fast disappearing, replaced by modern bungalows with corrugated iron roofs and the occasional two-story building. As new houses face the roads, the boundaries between the compounds of descent groups become difficult to trace. A bustling market place with its lorries, and the shops lining the main thoroughfares give an impression of both great economic activity and the rapid disintegration of traditional social structure.[10]

Since, as we have seen, Nigerian marriage and family life were based upon economic cooperation among members of the same kinship group, the disorganization of the traditional Nigerian family has affected the organization of labor in the Nigerian villages. The most obvious effect of family disorganization appears in the fact that the migration of men to mining and industrial centers and cities has placed the burden of agricultural production upon women and boys.[11] This has generally resulted in decreased production, since, with the disorganization of the traditional family system, the absent man's kinsmen do not feel the obligation to aid his wife. The less obvious but nonetheless important effects of the decay of the traditional family system on the organization of labor come to light when one studies the relation of the family to the economic life of the village.[12] In the African village the household is the economic unit within which the husband with his wives and children cooperate in gaining a living from the soil. The husband, who acts as the head of the household, may plant a garden for his wives and provide them with a granary. There is a division of labor based upon sex within the household as well as in the village. Sometimes men and women form separate groups to carry out the division of labor between the sexes.

Migration to urban centers has affected the age and sex distribution of the rural population. It has always been the young men who have left the village to seek wages, or sometimes adventure, in the mining camps and freer life of the cities. Consequently, it has been the old men, women and children who have been left behind to carry on the traditional life of the villages.

Today, much of the cash income of the rural areas finances the new social services—the schools, dispensaries, and a variety of benefits provided by the local government. These employ literates whom one might expect to be powerful agents of change in the communities where they work. Their education has alienated them from traditional society to a greater degree than that experienced by illiterate but wealthy traders.[13] Yet most of them work in communities other than those into which they were born. As employees of a missionary body or government they have been subject to frequent transfers. They have little opportunity to develop permanent relationships with those among whom they work. They are regarded as strangers by the local people and seek companionship among men of similar education and status. Their impact, beyond the compass of their employment tends to be small.

The literate living in his home town is not always in a better position to influence his community. His status is ambiguous. As a teacher or clerk, his loyalty to his employer is seen to conflict with that to his descent group or village. If he is a farmer, people ask why he has not made better use of his education; if a letter writer, a public scribe, he is seen as fomenting disputes, as profiting from litigation. Where literates are few in number, they are frequently afraid to press for changes, lest they be blamed for any untoward results. While the illiterates may be glad of his advice in setting up a new school, the literate man, usually quite young, lacks the authority to recommend higher taxes needed to pay for it. One important result in the rapid increase in the scale of social services in rural areas during the past decade is the greater number of local men who staff them. When the Yoruba town seeks to establish its own secondary grammar school, it puts pressure on the locally born university graduate to head it. Such men become drawn into local affairs far beyond their official spheres.[14]

Urban Life

Professor Rose Hum Lee has alluded to "the dominant role cities have played in initiating and perpetuating changes in behavior patterns and institutional organizations." [15] In much of the literature on African Urban life written in the past three decades, the terms "urbanization" and "detribalization" are freely used. In leaving his village society, the African becomes "detribalized"; in learning the new norms and values of town life, he becomes "urbanized." But these concepts have tended to obscure the degree to which relationships in the town may still be patterned according to traditional norms. The migrant, taking employment as a laborer in a large company or government department, must learn the behavior appropriate to bureaucratic structures. But on arriving in the town, he will not probably have lodged with distant relatives or other people from his home community, and his behavior toward these will follow that of the village. With every new contact that he makes, the immigrant has the choice between patterns of behavior from his village days and some new pattern.

Generalizations about life in urban society tend to stress the superficiality, anonymity and the transience of personal relationships, contrasting this with the dense network of close personal relationships to be found in a small and self-sufficient village community. The former generalizations seem in fact to be most appropriate to middle class suburbs of western industrial cities, and especially those of recent rapid growth; the slums of the old cities have quarters which are in social structure not unlike African villages. The Nigerian town cannot easily be divided into compact territorial sub-units, each encompassing persons in a restricted socio-economic status. Indeed, to the individual immigrant, the city presents a wide range of opportunities. He can, as many of the illiterate and unskilled workers do, maintain social relationships, save for those of the workplace and market, only with members of his ethnic group or home community. On the other hand, he may consciously exploit to the full the opportunities offered by town life, rejecting relationships with kin and past friends when these seem to be a handicap to further achievement. In Nigeria, town dwellers rarely resort to this means for the literate town dweller, in almost all cases, maintains fairly close links with his village of origin. Neither town nor village rejects the life of the other. Instead, the residents of each continually adapt their behavior to every new situation.

What are some of the outstanding characteristics of the Nigerian urban life? It may be right to say that the increasing population concentration shares a number of characteristics with urbanization in other parts of the world. The life of a city is complex—as it must be, since it draws to it people from many ethnic and geographic backgrounds. It is dynamic, since the growth process in itself creates changes to which people (and social patterns) must adjust.

On the whole, therefore, the new towns are peopled by recent migrants who are creating, by their presence, completely new patterns of relationship. Today the village houses have been given corrugated iron roofs, and a few shops often overlook the traditional market. In the capital, architects, released from the need to match their building with the existing styles, have designed some of the most exotic of modern buildings. Governments, anxious to provide visible expressions of progress both for their own people and for visitors from abroad, have spent freely on public construction.

In these towns a completely new range of occupations is open to

the migrant from the rural areas. New associations develop to pro-
tect these new categories of workers. The cinema, the bars and
night clubs provide entertainment unknown to the village. The extreme of affluence and poverty exist side by side in the town as new
forms of social stratification develop. Only in these towns is the educated and wealthy elite community of sufficient size for its members to effectively define new values and patterns of behavior.[16]   The town is the focus of political life. It is here that the nationalist parties developed. The leaders, in power today, are far
more influenced by pressures from the urban elite or by strike
threats from the workers than by rumblings of discontent in the villages. The congregation of the elite and of the workers in so few
urban settlements clearly stimulates their organization into groups
expressing their respective interests.

It is not surprising, therefore, that the town is the focus of inno-
vation. Here the individual may escape the restraint of family and
kin, of traditional elders and tribal values. He strives to improve
himself by looking relentlessly for a job or learning a trade. In
short, the urban migrant seeks to turn his rising expectations into
realities. How many men choose to do so is another matter; for, as
it has been noted, the Nigerian townsman tends to remain in a very
close relationship with his kin and community of origin.

The rate of growth of the urban population over the past three
decades has been approximately double that of the population as a
whole, most because of influx of migrant wage labor in search of
money needed to procure the growing numbers of goods and services which are becoming commonplace in rural as well as urban
life. The population of Lagos has tripled for the past 25 years, and
over half of it consists of persons born in other parts of the country.
The rapid growth of urbanization poses several socio-economic
problems. Housing, sanitation, and health facilities are unable to
keep up with it, resulting in the creation of large slum areas in the
cities. It has uprooted many of the people, mostly men, from their
traditional environment and placed them in a comparative and individualistic setting with which most of them are unaccustomed.

Buchanan and Pugh have given an adequate picture of Nigerian
urban communities by describing them thus:

> From the broadest possible point of view the towns of Nigeria fall
> into two generic groups: those that are largely European-created,

and those in which the urban nucleus is basically indigenous. The former are atypical and contain only a fraction of the country's urban population, though, since they include several important administrative centers such as Minna, Jos or Kaduna, they possess an importance out of proportion to either their numbers or their population. Their gridded street—patterns suggest their alien origin, but this external and invisible design contrasts sharply with their formlessness from the human standpoint . . . In contrast to the European-inspired centers are the old indigenous settlements, such as the Yoruba or Hausa towns, whose closely packed, closely peopled houses of red mud seem to spring originally from the landscape. Here, as in the tropical forest, is a perpetual cycle of decay and renewal, houses crumbling down into red laterite mud after a short, crowded life and others springing up incessantly to take their places. The complex intermingling of housing, small-scale industry and shops, the labyrinth of unpaved roads and alleyways, loosely confined between high compound walls, and the frequent absence of any dominating feature, convey an impression of shapelessness in appearance only . . . Half a century of European administration has not only greatly modified the internal structure of these towns; it has, however, led to the grafting on to the indigenous nucleus of a new commercial and administrative zone where the European trading concerns are established, along with the offices of various government departments, the police-station, and, where present, the railway station and the cinema. This newer zone will also contain the new and better class African housing and the settlements of non-native Africans, such as the Hausa and Nupe settlements in the southern city of Ibadan or the Yoruba settlements in the northern city of Zaria. Still further out and isolated from the indigenous city by a broad belt of bush is the government Reservation, where most of the European population and the higher rank African officials live.[17]

Generally speaking, it is the cream of the Nigerian elite who reside on government reservations or in other official housing, while the lesser elite find residential quarters, usually of far inferior quality, in the traditional nucleus. The latter neighborhoods lack the quietness of the suburban area and the attractiveness of the spacious, well-kept official quarters, with their garden and half-surface roadways.

Nigerian urban communities consist essentially of a multiplicity

Table of Some Nigerian Cities Showing
Their Population Growth from 1953–1963

Cities	Population* 1953	Population** 1963
Lagos	267,407	665,246
Ibadan	459,196	627,379
Ogbomosho	139,535	343,279
Mushin	32,079	312,063
Kano	130,173	295,432
Oshogbo	122,728	208,966
Abeokuta	84,451	187,292
Port Harcourt	58,846	179,563
Zaria	53,974	166,170
Ilesha	72,029	165,822
Onitsha	76,921	163,032
Iwo	100,006	158,583
Kaduna	38,794	149,910
Enugu	62,764	134,550
Aba	57,787	131,003
Ife	110,790	130,050
Benin City	53,753	100,694

* SOURCE: Population Census of Nigeria, 1952–1953. The 1952/53 Census dates were: North, July 1952; West, and Lagos, Dec. 1952; East and Cameroons, June, 1953. The total for Nigeria is 1953 Mid year estimate.
** SOURCE of 1963 Census data: *Demographic Yearbook, 1965,* New York, United Nations, 1966, P. 141. Note: The 1963 census data were supposed to be contraband.

of diverse social and cultural groups. Their populations have congregated rapidly by continuous, but often temporary, migration from both neighboring and distant areas. They are heterogeneous at several levels. Within the major "racial" divisions of Europeans, Asiatics and Africans there is heterogeneity according to occupations and ways of life. Among the Europeans, functional and social distinctions multiply between administrators, entrepreneurs, professional men, technicians and skilled artisans. Among Asiatics there is a wide range from small up-country traders to owners of large businesses and members of professions. Although among African migrants the diversity is not generally so great, it, too, is increasing. Even in new centers of primary industry (for example,

Nkalagu in the East, Lokoja in the North) Africans are no longer entirely confined to unskilled labor. Skilled artisans, large as well as petty traders, and in some centers substantial land owners and professional men are emerging.

The main "racial" categories have tended to remain closed social groups, the members of which interact with each other only in the technical and economic nexus of commerce and industry. Here the relations between Europeans, Africans and Indians are impersonal and according to set patterns. With the growth of sub-groups within the racial categories internal cultural barriers develop. This is seen where both, for example, "lower class" Europeans (especially Italians) are recruited as artisans and clerks into the increasingly complex system of industry and commerce, or where Africans achieve affluence and the Western standard of life.

Underlying these tendencies is the important fact that the component groups are severally associated with distinct external societies, whites and Asians with overseas homelands, classes and castes; African migrants with their tribal communities. Marriage, the education of children and the satisfaction of aesthetic and emotional needs are still linked with these homelands, and the divergent interests tend to perpetuate the separation of groups, reducing not only the social relations between them but also their adjustment and sense of obligation to the urban aggregate in which they live. Intergroup cooperation is, as suggested above, predominantly in the context of large-scale production, transportation and exchange with a Western apparatus. For all, including the Europeans, the activities and relations involved have been learned in adult life and are often only superficially, if at all, linked to the basic comprehension and attitudes acquired in early upbringing. Being more strongly internalized and retaining great emotional significance, the latter tend to predominate over obligations and opportunities for cooperation in work. This underlies the recurrent and intractable "misunderstandings" and mutual recriminations among officials, supervisors, clerks and "hands" concerning the lack of "explanation" and "consideration" on the one hand, or of industry "responsibility" and loyalty on the other.[18] In short, the cultural patterns of the urban technical system are sufficiently integrated to achieve construction and production, but are not themselves adequately integrated with the basic culture of the several categories and subgroups that it brings together. For the African in particular his life in the job is divorced not only from his childhood experience but also that of his home, neighborhood and tribe, and the values of the two milieus are often highly discrepant.

Transience is also characteristic of a large proportion of all the personnel in the several categories and groups. People are only temporarily associated with one another, all being migrants in greater degree, and expecting to reintegrate later in societies outside the urban area in which they are working. The cultural patterns and the social structures of the several groups, both major and minor, tend accordingly to be not only divergent and discontinuous but self-perpetuating. These structures and sub-cultures are furthermore ill-adapted at the outset to African urban conditions that are derived from parent patterns developed in more homogeneous contexts. This, though less apparent, is often as true for Europeans and Asians as for Africans. For the African worker in particular, who has been adapted in childhood to work and recreation in a comparatively small but comprehensive face-to-face group, the transition to a series of discontinuous impersonal relations—with employers, workmates, officials, landlords, policemen, and traders —is abrupt indeed. The craft and other skills he acquired in early life are often useless or at least undervalued in urban conditions. The early patterns of domestic kinship and neighborhood relations are often excluded, while the self-reliance and group-solidarity for shared production and sustenance under a subsistence economy are little guide to the foresight, economizing and bargaining required in the new patterns of wage income and the need to buy most goods, while unfamiliar modes of expenditure for livelihood and display are offered and even enforced.

On the whole the Nigerian town is indeed a society in course of construction, often empirically and with the help of "makeshifts," while at the same time it serves as a center to which many traditional, social and culture patterns are brought to be transformed or to fall into disuse.

It is in the towns that the methods of exploiting and administering wealth and the economic measures introduced by the colonial power can be seen at their maximum stage of development. Towns therefore provide an ideal field for any study of the effect of such measures upon society or upon the individual, or of circumstances which assist or impede technological process and modernization.

Finally, there can be no doubt that such unsettled, shifting ground can yield much new material for consideration by the sociologist. We are confronted here by a changing situation, demanding an essentially dynamic conception of social and cultural factors.

IV
GOVERNMENT
AND INDUSTRIALIZATION

Before the advent of Europeans, there was no central government which embraced all the regions in Nigeria as is the case today. Each tribe had its own informal government; some (like the Ibos) had no central authority or kingdoms like the Hausas and Yorubas. People were mainly subsistence agriculturalists as well as traders. Paul Bohanan raises the point that there was an active trade between the Africans (in our case Nigerians, especially the Hausas and Yorubas, because of their Kingdoms and external economic contacts and constant Arab invasion), Arabs and Indians, during the Middle Ages. The channels of trade were across the Indian Ocean and across the Sahara—even across the Mediterranean.[1] The small surplus produced by the farmers sustained, among some peoples (for example, Hausas, Yorubas, Effiks) a body of specialist craftsmen and of political and ritual office-holders. In other ethnic groups (Ibibios) crafts were carried out by men who were principally farmers; the village priest worked his land as did any other man. Intertribal contact was as a result of intertribal wars as well as economic factors as described above. So there was not much cooperation among the different tribes. But with colonialism (industrialization) there was a need for centralized government to integrate the different tribal groups. There was a shift, therefore, from informal, unstructured government as was in the East and oligarchic forms of government as was in the West and North, to a formal, well-defined form of government. Accordingly, the government role also shifted from mere prosecution of religious and intertribal wars to total governmental plan of the economy for the betterment of all the citizens. Hence, the government role now follows the pattern described below.

Traditionally, certain functions have been regarded as belonging to the government of any country pursuing a policy of industrialization. These can collectively be described as the fostering of an industrial climate, and may be divided into four very broad headings; namely, to ensure political stability, to promote dignity for work in industry, to create economic stability, and, as far as foreign private direct investment is concerned, to introduce incentives to foreign investors.

Political Stability

This first condition is sometimes the most difficult to attain. Until a country can boast of a good government, able to maintain peace, law and order, industrial growth will remain a dream. In Africa in the years 1962–1963 alone there were reported attempts to overthrow governments in the following countries: Ivory Coast, Dahomey, Tunisia, Nigeria, Ethiopia, Ghana, Sudan, Algeria, Senegal, the Congos, and Togo (this list is by no means exhaustive). Then in 1966 and 1967, a wave of coups in which the army took over government swept through Africa, especially West Africa. Hence whereas the great powers are to defend themselves against military attack from each other, the developing countries have to arm themselves against internal subversion sometimes controlled and directed from outside. Though it is regrettable that so much of the scarce capital badly needed for economic growth has to go into internal security and defense, it is nevertheless necessary to preserve order in society if an investment climate is to be created. It was with this in view that in Nigeria defense and security were later added as a fourth priority in the Six Year Development Plan.[2]

It must be mentioned however that despite these stability attempts industrial growth has been painfully slow. The Six Year Development Plan, 1962–1968, aimed at increasing the growth rate of the economy from 3.9 per cent to at least 4 per cent per year, is quite meagre.[3] This aim, rather modest compared to, say, Ghana's target of 7 per cent, was to be achieved by investing 15 per cent of the gross domestic product. At the same time, the per capita consumption was to be raised by about one per cent per year. The plan's long-term objective was to achieve self-sustained growth not later than by the end of the third or fourth National Plan.[4] The rate of domestic savings would have to be raised from about 9.5 per cent of the Gross Domestic Product in 1960–61 to at least 15 percent by 1975. More broadly, its aim was to increase opportunities, expand manpower training in all fields and at all levels, create major jobs in the nonagricultural occupations, modernize agriculture and foster Nigerian business.

The plan did not work well because of political instability. Right from the start of the military regime in 1966, investors held back from uncommitted expenditure in Nigeria. As the troubles of the new regime increased, culminating in the July countercoup and its bloody aftermath of massacres, investors' caution must have seemed to them only too justified. After the October 1966 riots in the North and East, the resultant mass emigration of Ibo from the North and Hausa and Yoruba from the East, and finally the civil war, official and commercial activity was seriously disrupted.

Cultivating Industrial Dignity

A second aspect of securing the right industrial climate is an environment which favors the entry of some of a country's best talent into industry. Social status in Nigeria has been too strongly weighted toward those in politics, law, and the top level Civil Service. If a country fails to accord social status to those engaged in technology, science and industry, then her industries cannot but attract the second best.

Nigerian educational systems and social standards have not given due dignity to manual work—yet the real need is to educate the public to recognize their increasing dependence on science and technology. Why is this so? For generations the Nigerian has associated social status, the exercise of responsibility, security and the means of enjoying Western material standards of comfort with government employment. Furthermore, up to the present time, the existence of only a few local industries has given little opportunity for Nigerians to develop managerial skills and little incentive to seek technical qualifications. The combination of these factors tend to inhibit the flow of persons with requisite standards of general education into industry and commerce and into private business.

To demonstrate how the educational system degrades manual work, we shall turn to the content of the school syllabuses before and after independence and compare their relevance to the Nigerian situation. In a report submitted for the Imperial Education Conference, 1913, the program of study in infant schools covering five classes, provided for instruction in religion, and nature study in vernacular for the first three years, with English being introduced as a subject in the fourth year. In addition, provision for kindergarten activities was prescribed. In the primary schools, in addition to continuing instruction in religion, nature study, hygiene and sanitation, geography and history were also taught. The optional subjects were singing, typewriting, shorthand and manual or agricultural training, but physical exercises, moral instruction, and humanities were compulsory subjects in all classes. This was sowing the seed of dislike for manual work. It is a psychological phenomenon that human nature tends to rebel against things forced upon it. Indeed, we have noted how some elites have become agnostics and anti-religious because of their gruelling experience of having to do religion all through their primary and secondary courses. The syllabuses before independence were retained after independence.

At the secondary school level, the report stated that education was in its infancy. A secondary school was defined as "a school or department of a school in which the subjects prescribed for such schools are taught, and for the proper teaching of which there is, in the opinion of the Directory of Education, an adequate staff." There were, in fact, eight such schools during this colonial era. Apart from the Hope Waddell Institute in the Eastern Province at Calabar, and the Abeokuta Grammar School, not then recognized by the Department of Education, all the secondary school provision was to be found in Lagos.

The object of the single government-sponsored school, King's College, "was to provide for the youth of the Colony a higher education than that supplied by the existing schools, to prepare them for the matriculation examination of the University of London, and to give a useful course of study to those who intend to qualify for professional life or to enter Government or mercantile service." In addition to the normal school program, the college held evening classes for apprentices for young men and women who wished to improve their general education, and for clerks requiring instruction in bookkeeping and shorthand. These offerings were without question related to the interests and needs of a small but significant sector of the community. But in so far as the content of the syllabuses was prescribed by the examination of the University of London, and which did not at that time provide special papers based upon local material, the courses were hardly relevant to the local environment.

Adverse criticisms were made by Nationalist leaders of the contents of the syllabuses, in particular, on the emphasis upon British history and geography, and the approach based upon the role learning of facts such as lists of the Kings of England, names of rivers, mountains and their heights. But it must be noted that these criticisms were rarely accompanied by any constructive alternative proposals even after independence. For example, in 1961, the commission appointed to review the educational system of Western Nigeria found it necessary to be extremely critical of the syllabuses and the educational system as a whole. In the forefront of their criticisms of the primary schools were the themes that primary education alienates the child from its environment, and that rural primary school leavers migrate to the towns in search of pen-pushing jobs for which they are not trained. Whilst they found that on the whole the syllabus for nature study, gardening and health was satisfactorily related to local conditions, they recorded their opinion that:

> There was very little sign of a development of lively curiosity and a desire to know about the immediate environment and the world outside. One got the impression that the pupils were just sponges imbibing knowledge not understood or digested, for the sole purpose of 'regurgitating' it for examinations.[5]

They did not find any wish to acquire practical skills, nor did they find respect for the value of manual work. They came to the conclusion that all the pupils wanted was to become junior clerks in offices because of the social status attached to office work. On gardening, the commission remarked, "We are told that some of the teachers use gardening as a form of punishment for the pupils." This could be the basic explanation for school-leavers' disgust for manual labor.

When they turned their attention to the secondary modern schools which had been inaugurated in 1955 to provide the key to vocational and professional training at the lower levels, they found it necessary to record a situation as depressing as they had found in the primary schools. Despite the detailed content of the syllabus which consisted of mathematics, nature study and biology, civics and history, geography, English and English Literature, arts and crafts, rural science, woodwork and light metal-work, home economics, needlework, elementary bookkeeping and elementary commerce, the commission had to report thus:

> Very few of the modern schools which we saw had adequate staff and few indeed offered any of the vocational courses. At the moment most of them only offer the purely academic course which provides only a 'polishing' of the education received at the primary school. Some of them are beginning to offer commercial subjects, but none of the schools we saw had the equipment to do metal-work and wood-work and there was very little evidence of rural science and art and handicrafts.[6]

Their criticism of the secondary grammar schools was brief, but to the point.

> The only serious criticism of the secondary grammar school is the neglect of any technical or practical education. At present, secondary school boys seem to have been groomed to think of themselves as being too good for any sort of manual work. It was observed that even the science learnt is very much out-of-date laboratory science and not related to their environment or in keeping with modern scientific knowledge.[7]

In conclusion, the commission suggested that the major reason for the failure to develop other forms of education more adequately than the conventional secondary school was due to the fact that the first Western schooling brought to Nigeria was a literary education, and that once "civil rule was established the expatriate administrators were graduates, most of them graduates in arts. And so the literary tradition and the University degree have become indelible symbols of prestige in Nigeria; by contrast technology, agriculture, and other practical subjects, particularly at the sub-professional level, have not the slightest esteem."

One of the major difficulties at the present time, as it has been in the past, in the planning of vocational training is the lack of information. The Federal Advisory Committee on Technical Education and Industrial Training in 1959 had to record:

> Our task has been complicated by the lack of detailed information concerning training requirements of some employers . . . It appears that a number of employers are unable or reluctant to plan ahead for their training needs and have submitted figures without much thought or consideration to future development. Some employers failed to make any return.[8]

In consequence of this, planning of vocational education and training as enunciated in the various reports and proposals published is still being expressed in general terms of establishing different types of vocational and training institutions rather than in specific real targets. Alternatively, they are directed to specific individual projects without reference to the education system or the economy as a whole. This situation will not change until the Federal and the State Manpower Boards are able to provide reasonably acceptable estimates of demands both for the public and the private sectors of industry, commerce and administration and in public service.

Two other considerations must be kept in mind when reflecting upon the provision of technical vocational education throughout this period. The first is the fact that both commercial and government organizations requiring the services of a labor force with varying kinds of skill followed the tradition of the craft industries in Britain with some form of apprenticeship or on the job training. Secondly, the demand for workers with a high degree of advanced technical and theoretical knowledge was small, but it is expanding. Furthermore, such industrial development as is likely to take place will call for training for adaptation to changing skill needs rather than for the specialized crafts where a man once having learnt his craft will practise that craft alone for a lifetime.

Yet the network of vocational and technical training so far developed, consisting of post-primary trade centers, technical institutes and an engineering faculty in one of the universities is still geared essentially to the methods and content of a system established in Britain in the nineteenth century. Something of this problem and the inadequacies of the whole educational system were fully revealed in 1960 when the Report of the commission on Post-School Certificate and Higher Education in Nigeria was published. The commission had been set up by the Federal Government "to conduct an investigation into Nigeria's needs in the field of Post-School Certificate and Higher Education over the next twenty years." The commission consisted of three Nigerians, three Americans, and three British. The Report is commonly referred to as the Ashby Report after the chairman of the Commission, Sir Eric Ashby. Details of the Commission are not necessary in our context.

The Federal Government has to take other steps besides the Commission proposals to correct the educational system. The people must be shaken out of their misplaced and false sense of tradition and self-satisfaction in the midst of want and poverty, into a mental reawakening to the greater possibilities which lie within their reach. Publicity and information organs must be reorientated to take note of the changes in technology happening both in Nigeria and outside. Much of the meagre publicity given to science and industry is handled by amateurs and free-lancers. This approach to a subject so important must be remedied by a more serious and concerted attempt to engage expert writers and commentators who can produce more effective messages for the masses. Since the government owns almost all the media of communication, this task falls automatically on it.

Economic Stability

The most important aspect of economic development depends on government economic policy toward foreign exchange. If a country has not enough foreign exchange as well as loans with which to buy imports of capital goods needed for industrialization, then industrial growth may well be unattainable. There is a growing body of opinion that there is an inherent long-term adverse balance of trade in the process of economic development in an underdeveloped economy. In Nigeria post-second World War growth has resulted in the worsening of the balance-of-payment situation and over a six-year period following 1955 the trade deficit increased by fifteen times.[9] Imports have generally grown faster than incomes. For example, while the gross domestic product at current prices in Nigeria in the 1950's was growing at an annual simple average rate of

8 per cent, imports were growing at 15 per cent, whilst exports were growing at 6 per cent. While imports remained relatively steady at about 15 per cent of the gross domestic product during the decade in question, exports have declined from roughly 20 per cent in the early part of the decade to about 12 per cent in the latter part.[10] Given this trend, it is evident that with the increasing import of capital goods which industrialization will call for, added to increasing loans commitments, Nigeria may be faced with difficulties in obtaining enough foreign exchange, thus imposing severe restraints on the growth of the gross domestic product.

To avoid this, economic planners have proposed certain steps to follow. Government economic policy should seek to increase the export of existing and new primary commodities, unprocessed, processed, or partly processed. On the import side, fiscal policy should seek to discourage import of consumer goods where there are opportunities for alternative domestic production. The consumption of luxury goods should be discouraged. This should be part of a general effort to raise domestic savings.[11]

The government realizes the economic shortcomings mentioned above and thus it has formulated policies very similar to those proposed by the economic planners. Because of the low per capita income, the federal and regional governments depend heavily on indirect taxation—mainly duties on foreign trade. The fiscal relations of the former regional governments are set forth in the Constitution (now being revised). The Constitution lists permissible sources of revenue and specifies activities for which public funds may be spent by the respective governments. Each regional government has a ministry of finance, independent and dependent (upon the Federal Government) sources of revenue,[12] and an annual budget approved by the legislature. Negotiation of loans from foreign governments lies mostly within the jurisdiction of the Federal Government. The proceeds of such loans may be used for federal purposes or may be reloaned to the regional governments.

The equilibrium of government finances and of the economy as a whole is overly dependent upon the world market prices of cocoa, oil palm produce, and peanuts. The stability of a regional government's finances and the economy of a region is dependent partly on some mineral wealth and partly on one crop: in the former Eastern Region (which has been split into three states), oil palm produce and petroleum; in the former Northern Region, peanuts and zinc, tin and columbite; in the Western Region, cocoa; in the Mid-Western Region, oil palm produce, cocoa and petroleum.

The system of regional (or state) government marketing boards has tended to insulate the economy from fluctuations in world market prices. The boards have an export monopoly on cocoa, oil palm produce, peanuts, cotton, and soybeans. By purchasing export crops for a number of years at a price below the world market price, the boards were able to build up reserves which permitted them to pay prices which were more stable than those in the world market. In this way, producer income and the economy as a whole has been less subject to disruptive external economic forces.[13]

Industrial Planning

We deem it wise to treat industrial planning in general before we take a look at the Nigerian situation per se.

The size and pace of economic development required in developing countries in the face of increasing population and a widening of the gap between the *haves* and the *have nots* of the world are immense and require rapid mobilization of capital on a scale which only central public authorities can attempt. Even when this capital comes in the form of a loan to a country, the outside investor, whether a government or an institution, will want to secure the loan. It is only the government who can in general provide security for such projects.

The immense problem of lack of *know-how* in underdeveloped countries requires a full scale attack on education of a size that no private institution can either finance or find profitable to undertake. Great industrial enterprises have played a prominent part in major development in technology in the advanced countries. Companies like the Ford Company of America, A.S.E.A. in Sweden, I.C.I. and A.E.I. in the United Kingdom, to mention only a few, have made immense contributions to technology in their respective countries. It is idle for an underdeveloped country to wait until industries of such stature exist before action in the field of technology is taken.

Developing countries are, or should be, in a hurry to catch up with the advanced countries. They are seeking to telescope into the space of a few years the revolution which has taken the advanced countries a century or more to accomplish. They can't afford the luxury of the laissez-faire policy which characterized many of the Western countries in their period of economic awakening. All national resources must be mustered and given direction and purpose. This is the task of a central authority.

Another major factor which has established the place of central planning is the Soviet experience. Leaders of most underdeveloped countries have been impressed with the outstanding success with which the Russians transformed their economy from an underdeveloped one to one of first class economic power within a few decades. The advanced countries of the West are no less impressed with this spectacular achievement and many of them, including the United Kingdom and France, have latterly engaged in a large measure of central planning.[14]

The result of these developments is that a basic technique of economic planning is at least emerging after decades of experimentation. The over-all centralization of the original Russian system of planning is giving way to a happy blend of decentralization of activities and central control. The emphasis on private decision and motivation advocated by people like Bauer[15] is giving way to a large degree of central planning and control and the central determination of targets. There is now a ready acceptance of the view that in this technological age the race for scientific and industrial supremacy must be centrally directed.

In many underdeveloped countries planning has assumed a political importance. A government which does not initiate long-term planning is likely to be accused of "planlessness" and even find aid-giving governments and agencies unwilling to have anything to do with it. The advanced countries, however, have been guilty of giving the impression that lack of industrial resources is synonymous with backwardness. In order to shed what they regard as vestiges of backwardness, many developing countries have embarked on industrialization, and there is little doubt that many of the actions taken by many of their governments in the field of industry today have a political motive.

Role of Industrial Planning
in Economic Development

Industrial planning is not exclusively concerned with purely economic issues. Indeed, the economist has been responsible for creating the opposite impression. For example, the introduction to the Nigerian Six Year Development Plan contains a sentence: "Governments may govern, economists may plan, administrators may organize, but ultimately the execution of all plans . . . depends upon the response of the people themselves." [16] Where is the technologist in all this? The result of this commonly held notion is that for a long time now economists have had to try their amateur hands on fundamental questions of sociology, technology and even politics in their attempt to formulate industrial plans. The result has often not been very satisfactory. Bonne (1957) has defined the problem thus: ". . . for the determination of targets of development, a division of work is clearly necessary between the economists and various specialists." Later he added:

> As to the determination of the means to achieve the ends, economic as well as non-economic, there should be cooperation on the part of all social scientists concerned. It will be necessary to consider 'non-economic' means as well in order to obtain the ends.[17]

Another result of this monopoly by the economist is the exclusion of the technologist from amongst those whose specialist knowledge is used for formulating national plans. The economist sees the technologist as the man to supply him with basic figures and data, and to put into practice what he, the economist had planned. The net effect is that development plans, when it comes to industrial matters, show insufficient technological study.

The important conclusion to draw is that industrial planning is a highly practical exercise touching on fundamental questions of technology, sociology, trade unionism, education and so on. None of these can be solved merely in economic terms. Successful and realistic industrial planning requires the meeting of minds of several disciplines. From this we deduce the first principle, which is that an industrial plan must be the joint work of many specialists, not that of the economist alone.

In practice industrial planning and economic planning are so closely related and interdependent that very intimate consultations are required. But this should not be a basis for thinking that they are one and the same thing. Developing nations need new approaches to industrial planning in order to provide a distinction between it and economic planning. Reasons for this new approach are thus:

The first is the inadequacy of many plans in their treatment of the industrial sector. Because the work is done single-handed by the economist much of this treatment does not stand up well to technical scrutiny. It is one thing to ask a technologist to report, for example, on a steel mill, without informing him of the use to which his report will be put or briefing him on the implications, assumptions and policies involved. It is another thing to ask the same man to come along and join other specialists and bring his knowledge to bear on the wide repercussions—which many economists think the technologist is incapable of comprehending—to be expected from each alternative suggestion he makes. The result in each case will be different.

The economist is qualified only to provide the general economic framework; after that he should give the specialist in each branch of the plan a degree of freedom to produce a comprehensive scheme.

Secondly, lack of adequate specialist attention has often resulted in economic development plans shying away from a bold attempt to formulate objectives in physical terms. It is only when an industrial project has been studied in sufficient detail that the outflow of goods over the plan period can be concisely stated. There are two advantages in having physical targets stated in a plan for a country where the audience is largely non-specialized. For example, the layman in Nigeria is more likely to be impressed if he is told that so many bicycles are to be produced over the period of a plan, rather than that so many millions of dollars are to be spent on a bicycle factory. In the second place, where the response of the public is assured, supervisors in industry are more likely to explain the challenge to the workers if output targets are stated in physical terms.

The problems of presenting an industrial plan in physical terms are many. Many industrial projects take a long time to complete due not only to "general" delays but also to what may be called "characteristic" delays peculiar to the type of industry. Characteristic delays are prominent during project surveys, phasing of construction schedules, commissioning and weather changes. The knowledge and estimation of these delays, in terms of the physical as well as the capital investment implications, come by experience and are often based very much more on local conditions than on conditions in similar plans elsewhere. An economist charged with planning such projects cannot always make the type of allowances that an industrialist would, nor can he always elicit the right type of answers from the specialist in the field. Physical output targets and yearly capital commitments based on such insufficient allowances are bound to be unrealistic.

The correct estimate of physical output targets depends on an accurate estimation of that perplexing parameter known as capacity. The capacity of each industry must be clearly stated as net or gross. In each the figures for output will be different. They will be dependent on production conditions, limitation of operation, changes in efficiency, shift working and so on. Here again the broad economic planner is at a disadvantage.

A dilemma soon results from trying to treat industrialization purely in terms of the economic development plan. At some stage, the economic development planner is not sure how detailed his study of the industrial sector ought to be in order to maintain proper balance between all the sectors. For example, should the economic development model be concerned with output in each year of the Plan, industry by industry? Should details of raw materials, inputs, intermediate goods and so on, industry by industry, be included? These are clearly difficult questions since these figures cannot form a single figure for total industrial investment. Reddaway (1962) advocated the need for a full-scale industrial model:

> Either the Plan (referring to India's Economic Development Plan) must be specified in full industrial detail or some rule must be given whereby investment expenditures can be allocated between different industries. Fundamentally, of course, the latter problem has to be faced at some stage and the question is simply whether to make the answering of it . . . part of the problem set to the model or to assume that a rough solution has been reached outside the model and to regard the model as testing the consequences of this detailed specification of the plan.[18]

The answer is simply found in setting up an industrial model outside the economic development plan model.[19]

The last reason for advocating industrial planning is the peculiar position of underdeveloped countries like Nigeria. In the advanced countries of the Western world capital moves quickly into fields where industrial opportunities lie without much initiative or even encouragement from the authorities. In underdeveloped countries a large measure of initiative is required from the central authority in order to attract foreign capital. Besides incentives and other fiscal and monetary measurements required, the preparation of industrial projects which are likely to interest foreign investors, and the development of potential industrial opportunities, are responsibilities which lie with the central authority. Because of the scarcity of skilled personnel able to tackle this task, such activity should be centralized. A former Western Nigerian Government report stated the problem thus:

> Representatives of foreign countries and donors who have visited the Region indicated that more aid would have come into the country if adequate and detailed analysis of projects indicating cost and benefits to the economy could be got ready to 'sell' to their organizations.[20]

Principles of Industrial Planning

Economic development in an underdeveloped country is distinguished by the overwhelming importance of choice between alternatives, which because of limited resources must be made by large groups rather than by individuals. These alternatives may involve structural changes in social organization and even in social philosophy. Such choices are so basic that government must be able to give a lead to the planners in formulating the overall objectives. Of the many objectives of planning usually listed, four are probably the most important:

a) rapid increase in per capita income
b) high level of employment
c) equilibrium in balance of payments
d) use of natural resources

To many people it is not apparent that these objectives generally conflict. For example, if increasing per capita income is taken as the primary objective, additional employment can only be gained if the country is willing to give up some amount of additional income. If this loss is zero, then there can be no separate employment objective. Or if we take another example, the balance of payments objective is not actually a social objective but rather a technical limitation on an industrial plan.

It is to be expected that a Government after receiving advice from a planning agency, will decide the relative weights to be attached to each objective. Based on this, a set of quantitative priorities should be established. These should be simple so as to be easily understood. The advantages of establishing priorities are many. First, it gives a sense of direction and purpose to those who are governed, and enables them to understand and comment on what their government is trying to achieve. Second, it reduces the field within which extraneous and partisan factors influence plans and thus encourages consistency of policy, whilst it also enables the precise contribution of each project to the economy to be evaluated and known. Third, it gives the various government agencies a basis from which to direct their day-to-day operations toward the achievement of the country's overall objectives. Fourth, it should also help to remove the prevalent impression that priorities are determined by the relative amount of money voted for different projects. Fifth, in order to determine the level of incentives to be given to a prospective investor in terms of pioneer status, level of protection and tax concessions, the industrial priorities enable responsibility for decisions to be delegated to the industrial planning agency on a routine basis without reference to a higher authority such as a cabinet, except for special cases that call for new directives of policy. This prevents delays in giving answers to industrialists' inquiries and encourages action and initiative at lower levels.

As the economy gets more complicated and diversified, it will become more difficult to apply these quantitative priorities. But the case for their continued use will become less pressing as the economy nears the point of "take-off."

Another cardinal principle is to ensure the full participation of the citizens in formulating and executing the industrial plan. There should be nothing secret about an industrial plan; it is an attempt on the part of constitutional authority to get everybody to achieve a certain target. It follows that a plan, right from its inception, should be as widely discussed as possible before being adopted as official policy. The attitude of regarding a plan as a secret document, being prepared by wise men highly placed, to be released by the government as a final work, does not help in achieving this aim.

Coming to the plan proper, the first major principle is that it must have a three-range projection, namely, the long-range, the medium-range and the short-range. The strategic long-term aim of an industrial plan is to cooperate with all sectors in achieving economic independence as soon as possible. Based on this, the economic plan, as distinct from the industrial plan, of a developing country, must fix a point in time when it is expected that independence can be achieved. This need not be rigidly adhered to, but should be revised as occasion calls for it. With the long-term economic objective determined, the corresponding long-range strategy for industrial planning can be settled, followed by the medium-range and lastly by the short-range strategy. With these milestones adequately established, the structure and composition of the short-term industrialization program should be worked out in great detail. Reddaway (1963) calls this approach comprehensive planning done "backwards." By this, one chooses a definite date, five to ten years hence, and attaches to this date certain economic objectives; one then starts from the end products which one considers desirable to make available to find consumers (whether individuals or government, whether for immediate consumption or for securing future production or income) and sets out to deduce requirements of material, manpower, intermediate products, etc., required to meet this target, and then to see what has to be done in the intervening years.[21]

In the actual industrial planning exercise there is a basic objective, which is to analyze production possibilities, and from such analysis to choose from amongst several alternatives a pattern of industrial growth based on the overall priorities and policy directives issued by the government and the likely response from the private sector. For this reason, we see that it is possible to deduce a basic method of industrial planning which is capable of considerable variation.

Generally, industrial planning has three broad phases, namely, the aggregate analysis, sector analysis and commodity and project analysis. The aggregate analysis provides the vital link between industrial planning and overall economic development planning. It provides the framework for planning in all sectors of the economy. This is because estimates of national income, available supplies of capital, labor and imported goods are essential for projecting the growth of individual sectors of industry.

Sector analysis starts with estimates of final demands[22] for the different commodities. This exercise is usually confronted with many problems due to insufficient data and statistics, and in general much approximation has to be accepted. Estimates of final demands provide a basis for preliminary estimates of the related total industrial output. The next inquiry is to obtain estimates of intermediate demands. For this purpose, estimates of demands from other producers are added to, and estimates of imported commodities are subtracted from, the estimates of final demands, to give estimates of final industrial output. The estimate of total industrial output gives a first idea of the total amount of resources that the industrial development in the country will call for, and the idea of sector, commodity, and project analyses is to get the final amount of resources required to agree with the total industrial allocation. These exercises require some sort of inter-industry analysis. In a country which produces mainly consumer goods and also imports the bulk of its industrial material and machinery, inter-industry relations will be limited and the exercise is that much simpler.

The next part of the exercise will be the initial selection of the industrial sectors. In this initial selection, the following factors must be considered: amount and location of demand, cost structure of representative plants within the industry, transport and other costs, and the desirable long-term growth. The following main factors will determine the initial sector choice: labor and capital requirements, volume of demand in relation to scale of output of an efficient plant, saving in transport costs that may result from local production, and skills required. With this information, final selection can be made, again by applying the "industrial priorities" rules as approved by the government.

Project analysis then follows in order to select the best projects from each of the chosen sectors. For this is necessary to break down the original sector projections into demand for commodities. For example, in a Peruvian study, a sector of the international standard industrial classification entitled "Manufacture of metal products except machinery and transport equipment" was broken down into twenty-two commodities such as table and kitchen cutlery; nails, tacks and staples; lighting fixtures, etc. The use of this breakdown is to determine the demand for commodities produced by individual plants in order to examine their viability. It will be necessary to take account of such factors as the similarity in production process, similarity in the use of the final output and relative importance of the commodity in value terms.

This breakdown provides the information on which pre-project decisions can be based. It is also at this stage that the relative contributions of large-scale industry versus small-scale handicraft and cottage production can be determined. The same criteria used for industrial sector selection can be used for project selection, but instead of the analysis being based on typical plant techniques and costs, as before, emphasis should now be on the data for the various alternative plant layouts that are typically possible. The basic industrial priority criteria will again be applied as between each of these alternatives. It will be necessary here to take account of a number of industrial policy objectives, such as industrial location, defense, regional development and the relative role of private and public capital. These questions bear very heavily on social objectives. The scale of operation and production techniques will also feature prominently. For this purpose estimate of output variation over the planned period will be considered. The technical questions of how and whether to expand existing facilities, together with means of improving their efficiency and better utilization of installed capacity, for example, by double shift working and the effect of choice of technique on quality, will be taken into account.

A practical industrial plan must take account of the effects of existing projects and the limitations imposed on it by past decisions which cannot be changed even if it were desirable. Second, the plan must be detailed enough to ensure that all the projects are properly phased, since the complicated nature of inter-industry relationship may well mean some projects either cannot be used at all or cannot be used to the full extent as soon as they are ready because the complementary industries or services are not ready. Third, the factor limiting the target output of each industry must be considered. In general, the output of any particular industry will be limited by whatever one of the following three factors yields the lowest figure: (a) demand for the industry's goods and services, (b) supply of essential inputs (manpower, materials, capital), (c) industry's ability to supply, assuming (a) and (b) are adequate. According to Reddaway, a good plan will arrange for the limiting factor in each case to be the industry's ability to supply.[23] Fourth, the problems of social dissatisfaction make it obligatory that a plan in the final form must show that it has the interest of the common man in view. The industrial plan must therefore indicate, and indeed emphasize, its contribution to the rise in consumption and real value of income per head of population together with some systematic list of the principal consumer goods to be produced.

In summary:

a) Industrial planning must be a function distinct from economic development planning, though the former must be done in the context of the latter.

b) Industrial planning in an underdeveloped country must be on a national basis in order to take advantage of the economies of scale in a situation in which total purchasing power is still relatively small.

c) Industrial planning is a practical exercise requiring not only the economist but also other specialists.

d) It is necessary through all stages of planning to associate with it the people who will put the plan into operation. If possible let representatives in different sectors of industry criticize it before it is published.

d) Every effort should be made to reduce the influence of politics on industrial selection and location by adopting definite guide lines of policy. An important aspect of this is the evolution of an industrial priorities formula.

f) The planning exercise to be exhaustive must consist of a three-level analysis—namely aggregate analysis, sector analysis, project and commodity analysis. This analysis should be checked for consistency.

Industrial Planning

Realizing that the main hope for an expanding economy lay in increasing and diversifying production, the federal and regional gov-

NIGERIAN MAJOR TRADING PARTNERS Country	1964	1965	1966	1967*	1968*
			(*Imports* c.i.f.)		
United Kingdom	78,670	85,050	77,530	64,570	59,880
Other Commonwealth	15,910	17,910	16,620	13,360	12,000
West Germany	22,510	29,540	27,460	23,230	21,230
Italy	12,880	12,720	13,040	10,750	13,780
France	9,940	12,100	14,500	9,420	7,180
Netherlands	10,210	10,430	9,290	9,340	7,830
Belgium/ Luxembourg	3,330	3,430	3,510	2,900	3,280
Eastern Europe	7,030	7,290	6,460	8,010	8,730
China	3,130	4,860	5,020	6,260	3,720
Norway	4,850	5,720	6,760	4,560	2,110
USA	28,930	33,080	41,520	27,850	22,290
Japan	30,810	25,610	14,320	18,750	7,160
			Exports (domestic, f.o.b.)		
United Kingdom	80,660	101,460	105,180	70,320	61,940
Other Commonwealth	8,490	4,990	13,420	10,820	7,350
West Germany	26,900	27,860	27,760	25,570	18,190
Italy	7,470	10,940	13,660	14,110	13,120
France	10,000	18,240	25,910	22,420	11,540
Netherlands	27,050	31,540	26,100	30,790	27,040
Belgium/ Luxembourg	5,240	7,700	7,080	3,150	5,880
Eastern Europe	3,940	6,810	3,370	5,530	8,600
China	590	700	—	940	250
Norway	840	750	460	520	950
USA	14,320	26,210	22,330	18,480	16,040
Japan	2,570	3,160	4,250	6,140	3,660

* Provisional.

Note. Nigeria became an Associate Member of the EEC by signing an agreement in 1966; the French never ratified this agreement, however. In October, 1968, Nigeria repudiated this agreement.

This table is reproduced from: Colin Legum and John Drysdale, *Africa Contemporary Record: Annual Survey and Documents, 1969–70,* Exeter, Africa Research Ltd., 1970, p. B582.

ernments have inaugurated long-term capital development programs which are essentially five- to six-year economic plans. In
addition to establishing an economic infrastructure, the governments have set about training subsistence farmers in modern methods of production and introducing, through research, new crops,
and improved strains of established crops. Technical training facilities have also been set up to provide the skilled labor necessary in
establishing industries. Government development and finance cor-
porations have been created to investigate directly new industrial
and agricultural undertakings.

Development plans provide for a wide variety of expenditures on
items ranging from aviation to the development of veterinary services. Major emphasis, however, has been on roads, railroads, education, medical and health services, waterways and harbors, and
water supplies.[24]

Planning also searches for new markets for exports and attempts
to strengthen the existing markets. Nigeria has achieved spectacular success in signing bilateral trade agreements with a number of
Eastern and Western countries; increased inter-African trade has
also been accorded priority. Another point in planning is a concerted effort with other developing countries to obtain better terms
for trade in primary commodities. In pursuance of this objective,
Nigeria became a full member of the International Agreement on
Wheat, Sugar, Tin and Coffee and sent a strong delegation to the
1963 International Cocoa Agreement Conference. She has also
played a leading role in the establishment of two producer associations, namely the Cocoa Producers' Alliance and the African
Groundnut Council.[25] Planning also suggests steps to be taken to
stop large-scale remittances of capital to foreign countries. Particular fields in which this has threatened Nigeria's balance of payments were football pools and insurance. A government-sponsored
football pool has gone some way to stem the flow of pools' money
overseas. A national insurance company to cater initially for Nigeria's exports, together with the increasing opportunities now offered
to insurance companies in Nigeria to put their funds into useful investments in the country will, it is hoped, help to reduce this drain.
Another means that has been used to reduce the drain of "invisible" transactions is the transfer from London to Lagos of the selling organization of the Nigeria Produce Company; thus for the first

time Nigerian produce can be sold direct to other countries from Lagos.

Regionalism vs. Planning

We have already mentioned Walter Schwarz's comment that Nigeria's economic assets are offset by some serious liabilities, chiefly of a political nature. The federal structure itself has militated against rational, nationwide planning. While the Constitution reserved to the federal government the right to raise long-term loans abroad, short-term credits could be raised by the regions. The Six Year Plan (1962–1968) was drawn up separately in each region and then formally integrated.[26] A National Economic Council officially presided over a unified economy, but in practice the regions were economic rivals.[27] Each government, and indeed each minister within it, faced constant pressure for industries to be sited in the home territory, a pressure which increased in proportion to the ever rising rate of unemployment. Possibly the most flagrant example of this rivalry was the decision reached by the National Economic Council in May, 1964, that the proposed iron and steel industry, for which the Plan had set aside $90 million, should be split into two, with half of it sited in the North at Idah and the other half in the East at Onitsha. Indeed it was only after intense negotiations that a claim by the Western Region to have a share as well was rejected— and then only because at the time the West was the weakest of the regions in terms of federal politics.[28] However, the iron and steel industry is still in the talking stage and the 1964 decision can be reversed.

Too much economic independence in the regions has presented some new industries with the paradoxical threat of over-production. Among the first to feel it was the soft drinks and brewing industry. In 1949, when Heinekens and the United Africa Company joined in the first "Star" beer and soft drink venture, the import of soft drinks totaled around 2,000 gallons a year. In 1964 there were twelve full-scale plants in operation, with a capacity of 12 million gallons but actually producing only 4.5 million gallons. Instead of working two or three shifts, most were working three or four days a week and heavy losses were incurred.[29] The same problem arose in textiles. By 1966, eight plants had been built since independence and present planned capacity was 165,000 spindles and 4,600 looms—more than five times the pre-independence figure. Production capacity was 170 million last year, 1968—about 60 million more than the combined import and local production figure in 1964. Also production of cement in five major plants became very expensive because of mislocation, for example, Nkalagu cement factory.

This short review is intended to show that the financial policy of Nigeria is both unified and forthright, and has the basic constituents on which to build for industrial growth. The weakness in the Nigerian economic machine is that, having laid the foundation, the same vigor has not been shown in building the rest of the house. The industrial strategy of the various regions lacks coherence.

Government and Private Industry

The question to ask is what a government in a developing country can do to attract enough private capital from abroad, and what should such a government do in order to see that apart from making profits, private investors contribute as much as possible to the long-term economic and social progress of the host country. Furthermore, has a government any duty to play the role of a go-between with the private investor on the one hand and the public on the other?

In the highly competitive world market for capital, it is the borrower who has to make the move and it is for a government to create an atmosphere which encourages long-term investments. Experience has shown that the idea that all that capital wants in order to travel abroad is a fair return is wrong. Underdeveloped countries need to provide various incentives to foreign industrialists. (The Nigerian situation will be discussed in the next paragraph.) Apart from the initial provision of incentives, the government has a central role to play in meeting the changing needs of foreign industrialists as and when they arise, either by providing new types of incentives or by removing anomalies that may exist in the social or political field.

In Nigeria, a deeply liberal attitude to business and the absence of a strongly entrenched left-wing element in politics have also been a help to the authorities in attracting foreign investments. The

Federal Minister, the late Chief Festus Okotie-Eboh, said categorically in his 1965 Budget Speech:

> Nigeria's need today is not for doctrinaire theorists importing foreign dogmas that have little relevance for Nigeria, but for men of initiative, men with ideals, planners and thinkers, the kind of men whose pioneering vision, allied to faith and plain hard work, built the United States, the Great Britain and the Canada that we know today.[31]

He was challenged in Parliament for making this statement. He was, after all, a member of the "National Council of Nigerian Citizens" (NCNC) which was a socialistic political party at least in name if not in practice. In reply to his critics Chief Festus explained blandly, and amid general satisfaction, that he had rejected only the "foreign imported brand," and not the "African indigenous brand"—which, he stressed, was evolutionary and not revolutionary.[31]

This official liberalism has been expressed in practical terms in the shape of generous incentives for foreign investors. These include liberal income tax and import duty relief, accelerated depreciation allowances and the imposition of protective duties and import quotas. The basic machinery for exchange control is on the statute book as a precaution but it is not applied; neither in the remission of profits nor in the repatriation of private salaries are there irksome restrictions.[32] Naturally, the large expatriate trading firms are encouraged to reinvest their profits in the country and this they have not been willing to do.[33] Although some of the companies which dominated foreign trade at the moment of independence have all withdrawn from the retail and produce-buying sides of their business, and reinvested the capital in industry. The giant United African Company, a subsidiary of Unilever, is now associated with a dozen industrial ventures, including brewing, plywood, vehicle assembly and textiles.[34]

Equally, the government acts as a middleman between the foreign investor and the indigenous private sector. In Nigeria, as in many underdeveloped countries, the resentment against what often looks like foreign domination of the economy is common, resulting in argument for nationalization of foreign-owned industries. Mr.

Nehru in 1963 called for what he described as "economic democracy" if the masses in India were not to get impatient and throw peaceful solutions to the economic and social problems of India overboard. This is the basic problem with which many underdeveloped countries are faced.

In Nigeria, the call to expatriate firms by the government to leave the retail trade to indigenous firms has met with reasonable response and has helped to alleviate the fear of foreign domination of the economy. Foreign companies have helped to establish a variety of industrial activities. In many cases, these factories send their goods for wholesale and retail sale to the sales organizations belonging to the same owners. This places the businessmen in a strong trading position especially when they make the goods they sell.

Government Financial Aid to Small Industries

A look at the United Nations policy on industrialization and productivity will form an adequate yardstick to judge the Nigerian Government performance in financial aid to small industries. The policy is as follows: any government which is interested in industrialization and productivity has to have the intention to encourage entrepreneurs to make use of their skills and indigenous materials in the establishment of new enterprises. Such a program would of course involve financial assistance, management training, technical training to provide productivity, assistance in locating or building efficient factory units and equipping them with the hand tools and machine tools needed. All this would be to no avail if there is no government procurement. Kennard Weddell in his article, "Promotion of Small-Scale Industries Through Government-Planning," [35] lists the steps Government procurement should follow to provide small industries with orders for articles and services.

1. Establishment of a small industries agency by the central government.

2. Careful screening by that agency, jointly with officials of the purchasing agencies of all articles and services the government intends to purchase. The purpose of this screening is to determine which article might be produced locally rather than imported.

3. Additional screening to determine the possibility of having these items produced by small independent enterprises rather than by large industrial concerns, regardless of whether these latter concerns are in the public or private sector.

4. The utilization of the practices developed and invoked by the small industries co-operating with the Government, to channel purchases of items which can be completely produced by small business to the previously inspected small enterprises. This can be done by making use of such preferential treatments as prices—differentials and small-business class set-asides.

5. A fair but reasonably simple definition should be established of what constitutes a small industrial concern. This definition should be flexible and should not discourage the growth of the relevant industrial concerns, either as regards the number of employees or the volume of productivity.

6. In the case of end-items which at the outset can't be satisfactorily produced by small enterprises and must be produced by large concerns, government sanction should be secured for a particular subcontracting program on the part of these latter concerns in the public or private sector, regardless of whether or not they have government contracts.

Although the above are based on just experience, each country's program should be "tailored" to meet its own specific conditions. The small industries should establish and maintain a close liaison with their counterparts and other newly industrializing nations for their mutual benefit.

Let us now consider the case of small industries in Nigeria. The reluctance of Nigerians to forsake trade for industry where returns are less assured underlines the lack of indigenous capital. On the other hand some advance in saving habits is to be found from post office savings bank records. In 1939, there were only 42,737 accounts, whose savings totaled $555,000; in 1961 the number of accounts was 287,672 and the amount deposited totaled $7,365,000.[36] To assist in the problems of finance the government enacted the Aid to Pioneer Industries ordinance in 1952. Under this any undertaking satisfying the condition that it is favorable to the Nigerian economy is granted a pioneer industry certificate and obtains various tax reliefs. A Federal Loans Board also exists to give moderate financial aid to industrial projects. These measures have helped to bring about a marked expansion in consumer goods industries in the last five years, especially at Lagos and Port Harcourt. There are now nearly forty factories on the Ikeja Industrial Estate near Lagos, manufacturing such products as tires and inner tubes, asbestos cement products and paints. On the United Nations Scale the government is not doing badly.

However, in the immediate future the process of development will depend to a large extent upon the role played by the educated elites—upon their size and their levels of education and training, and upon the ability of the leaders to analyze the problems facing the country. This task seems peculiar to the developing nations of the twentieth century; in the nineteenth century Western Europe, it was the craftsman and small entrepreneur who promoted industrial development, not the university graduate with his liberal education. But "the small size of these new elites," said P. C. Lloyd, "necessitates cohesion and enthusiasm among their members, but these will be vitiated by continual struggles for power between different groups or by the retreat of the frustrated into bureaucratic ritualism." [37]

Despite all hope for industrialization the Nigerian politicians realize that the country will remain basically agricultural for some time and that improved farming must be a major contributor to economic growth. Nigeria has established settlements for peasant farmers who might be expected to gain an income similar to that of a skilled artisan. Yet development of this type frequently requires as much capital investment for each participant as 20 manufacturing industries. W. Arthur Lewis writing in his "Reflections on Nigeria's Economic Growth" takes this standpoint:

> The more profitable agriculture becomes, the greater the likelihood that 55 per cent of school teachers will be willing to enter it (on the one hand) and also the greater will be the expansion of services, industries, and manufacturing, to absorb the remaining 45 per cent (on the other hand). If agriculture does not grow neither will transport, distribution, government services, nor (after the imported substitution stage is exhausted) manufacturing.[38]

The potential for agricultural development is the crucial element in this analysis. The technological possibilities are clearly immense but Sir Arthur feels that if they are to be fulfilled, there should not only be a drastic rise in overall investment in agriculture, with government spending much more on small-scale agriculture and much less on plantation than they now do, but there should also be much greater attention to incentives. While he extols the agricultural investment and improvement, he does not favor the present government policy on farm settlements. But if we examine the view of Frederick Harbison and his co-authors in "Industrialism and Industrial Man" [41] that "To the economic eye a community that needs to have a majority of its people working on the land is merely demonstrating its inefficiency," we may consider another solution. It might be better and more economical if both agricultural as well as manufacturing and extractive industries are improved simultaneously. The government's recent main objectives for the 1968–76 economic plan tends to be on these lines.

> The main objectives of the next plan will be a high overall rate of economic growth with a view to achieving 'self-sustained growth' before the end of the twenty-year Perspective Plan; the rapid industrialization of the economy; increased production of food for domestic consumption without relaxing efforts in the export sector; and a drastic reduction in the magnitude of the present unemployment problem. It is, of course, fully realized that all these objectives may not be entirely consistent.[30]

What will impede such a step to be taken in capital? The rate of capital formation in Nigeria, and thus the rate of industrialization, will depend upon the flow of public and private foreign capital into Nigeria, and upon the world price levels of the commodities which Nigeria exports—cocoa, palm oil, peanuts, minerals, cotton, rubber, and timber. The most important single internal source of development capital is the spread between the price paid to the producer by the marketing boards and the price the board receives in the world market for the export crops. If world prices are high the boards can keep the margin wide and invest funds in industrial projects; but when prices are low, the boards dare not reduce prices to producers in order to maintain the margin. Many agricultural producers are already convinced that Nigeria is being developed at their expense and that may be the reason why the government indulges in farm settlement investments so that the farmers will owe allegiance to it. Savings of individuals for the most part do contribute to the formation of investment capital.

On the part of government, therefore, its main goal in the plan for industrialization is a diversification of production in order to reduce dependence upon fluctuating world prices for a few primary products—oil palm products, peanuts, cocoa and cotton—which are about the source of the bulk of Nigeria's income. The situation is changing now with Nigeria exporting crude oil. However, the prestige which is thought to be associated with an industrial economy is not a negligible factor.

V

CHARACTERISTICS OF THE "ELITES," MIDDLE CLASS, AND WORKING CLASS

In a book published not many years ago, Toynbee made the prediction that future historians would say that "the great event of the twentieth century was the impact of the Western civilization upon all the other living societies of the world of today. They will say of this impact that it was so powerful and so pervasive that it turned the lives of all its victims upside down and inside out—affecting the behavior, outlook, feelings, and beliefs of individual men, women, and children in intimate ways, touching chords in human souls that are not touched by mere external material forces—however ponderous and terrifying." [1]

Whether or not future events will confirm Toynbee's prediction, there can be no question of the correctness of his own brief but vivid description of the profound effects of the impact of Western civilization on non-European peoples. Of the non-European peoples who have been influenced by Western civilization, none reveal so strikingly the changes described by Toynbee as the peoples of Africa and consequently the people of Nigeria. The problems created by this Western influence are both sociological and psychological—sociological in the broad meaning of the term, in as much as the impact of the West has, in Toynbee's words, "turned their lives upside down and inside out"; that is, it has destroyed the social forms in which the traditional "behavior, outlook, feelings and beliefs of individual men and women" were shaped and had meaning.

The leaders of the pre-colonial Nigerian Society (indeed African societies as a whole) were the chiefs and priests, the influential men, the wealthy traders;[2] and it was with such men—we may call them the traditional elite—that the early Europeans negotiated. Later in the colonial period these same men were often used in systems of native administration as instruments of colonial rule. Educated traditional rulers, sitting in councils of chiefs or on the governors' legislative councils, were apt to see themselves as heirs to British Power. The members of the traditional elite were, of course, recognized as such only in their own kingdoms and communities. They did not gain general recognition throughout the newly created colonial territories.

The Rise of the New Elite

Why, at this particular stage in history, did a new elite class develop? What undercut the supremacy of the traditional elite and gradually pushed forward the Western educated group?

> In view of the principle that a society values most those who serve the currently most prized social functions one may assume that the new elite somehow fits today's need better than do the old. It is these who have led the advance toward nationalism and independence, they who have answered with their achievements the contention that Nigerians are not ready to function in twentieth-century government and technology (though this contention is today partly true), they who have demonstrated a capacity to meet on Western terms the challenge of adaptation to the modern world. Nigeria has recognized these functions by giving deference to the new functionaries on a broader scope than ever before, cutting across tribal lines and developing new patterns of social alignments.[3]

It is not difficult that once there was such an elite group, society could recognize and value its contributions. But what accounts for the existence of this group?

An indigenous elite modeled on European lines has been in the process of formation since the earliest phases of colonial occupation.

The older nucleus of Western trained people was greatly expanded (as already stated) by the increased numbers of graduates of mission schools and by the return, after World War II, of those who had gained higher education overseas. The younger element showed themselves increasingly competitive and ambitious; their nationalist leaders and spokesmen sought more aggressively to open up the path for their advancement in government careers, which was linked to the collective goal of self-government and independence for the country. They aimed at replacing Europeans at comparable levels throughout the senior civil service, as well as gaining the prestige, political power, and incomes which would attach them to elective parliamentary and ministerial office. Nationalist political pressures also accelerated prospects of advancement to higher responsible levels in the large foreign business firms and hastened the handing over of local control in churches and mission schools. Politics and civil service careers are decidedly the main avenues of upward mobility which they exploited, as the former barriers were lowered and their educational qualifications rose.

Nowadays, another generation of elite has been produced by a diversification of the means of attaining an elite status. No longer is education almost the sole qualification; members of the political party in power (men who often through misfortune or lack of ability received little education) may rise to positions of considerable political power through their demonstration of loyalty to the party leaders and their influence over the masses. Thus the highly educated civil servant is resentful when his advice and decisions are challenged by party officials.

"Thus the rapidity of social change is producing in Nigeria a succession of elites with different criteria of achievement and a different set of values. And among these groups there is rivalry to control the political system of the nation," wrote P. C. Lloyd.[4] It is this interregional rivalry among the elites that precipitated the past civil war.

The new elite, therefore, can be defined as a variable group of people consisting at least of all who have completed upper secondary school (eleven or twelve years of formal education). On the lower levels these persons are the clerks and the teachers in lower secondary schools; on the upper levels, they are the professional and top-ranking government figures or the most powerful traditional rulers, for example, the emirs in the North. The top-level elite—the true elite in a narrower sense—shade into the lower elite levels or sub-elite since an elite family commonly contains both, and marriages and guest lists at social affairs commonly ignore any presumed boundaries between them. Mobility is high, and there is a common assumption that today's clerk may be tomorrow's prime minister.[5]

Characteristics

The characteristics of the emerging elite are—youthfulness; education which includes overseas training and degrees; urban living patterns and values which follow the European model; Christian, or occasionally, Moslem religious affiliation, and vigorous concern for Nigeria's national growth even though present incidents seem to forestall this characteristic. They affirm their pride in old ways to some extent, for instance, by wearing one of the forms of traditional dress, and they usually maintain their kinship obligations and loyalty to their specific places of origin.[6]

The old and new elite groups overlap and dovetail. In the growing urban communities, where old ways are constantly assaulted by Western influences, the modification of the old is greatest and the social demand for new kinds of leadership and new social functions is at its peak. It is in the cities that the new elite have ascended into positions whose prestige equals or exceeds that of the traditional rulers, who hold shrinking sway over that position of the social organization in which indigenous custom is dominant. In the North where the old is strongest and Western influence least pervasive, traditional rulers retain considerably more power than they do in the South, which is both more urban and more Westernized, and whose people are more politically conscious. In both North and South the traditional ruler is more secure in rural than urban areas.

What are the changes which are occurring in the personality of the Nigerian (or African) as the result of culture changes? Malinowski stated that the ethnographer could not "accomplish the task of sorting out a Westernized African into his component parts without destroying the one thing in him that matters—his personality—and that the educated African is a new type of human being, endowed with abilities and energies, with advantages and handicaps, with problems and visions, which neither his European neighbor nor his 'blanket' brother are heirs to." [7] Thus the personality which the African (here Nigerian) has acquired as the result of social changes should be regarded as one aspect of an organ's process involving an interaction between changes in the personality and changes in culture of the group.[8]

The first important effect on the Nigerian's personality of the changes resulting from industrialization seems to be the development of an individualism that was unknown in traditional African society.[9] As we have seen, in the traditional society the Nigerian was enmeshed in a web of social relationships, implying obligations and providing security, which left little room for the assertion of himself as an individual. "African society," writes Westerman, "is characterized by the prevalence of the idea of community." He adds:

> The individual recedes before the group. The whole existence from birth to death is originally embodied in a series of associations, and life appears to have its full value only in these close ties. Though there is in them a well-ordered gradation between persons who command and who obey, yet the prevailing feeling is that of equality. Class distinctions as we know them are absent or but feebly developed. They may be of greater weight in countries where there is a marked distinction between a ruling group and a subject people, but usually with a social unit the consciousness of a strong sense of solidarity is predominant. The group imposes duties on the individual but it also grants privileges; it takes from its members much of their personal responsibility and offers them its protection.[10]

The economic factors caused the development of individualism from the first contact that the Nigerian had with European industry. When he goes to work on a European plantation or farm or at the mines, "he receives wages as an individual; he pays tax as an individual . . . ; if he marries he finds the necessary cattle out of his own earning instead of relying upon the obligations of his clansmen or kinsmen to contribute."[11] Conversion to Christianity has tended to provide and reinforce a social and religious basis for the individualism that has resulted from industrialization (which itself is a result of European contact). The very act of becoming a Christian has generally meant an assertion of his individuality in opposition to group pressure. For, as Westerman has pointed out, "conversion is a personal matter, an affair between man and God. A man may draw his family with him, but, for them as for him, it is a personal step. When a person living in pagan surroundings adopts Christianity he often loses the protection or even membership of his group and has to stand by himself." [12]

As the Nigerian has been compelled "to stand by himself" in economic and social relations, he has been compelled to adopt a more rational attitude toward the world.

There are culture conflicts involved in the acquisition of Western culture which affect the Nigerian personal orientation toward the world. Conflicts may also arise from the Christian teachings. These conflicts are often related to the new conception of themselves as the result of Westernization. Under the old tribal system the African thought of himself as a member of a group that was bound together by kinship and communal ties. As the old tribal life is breaking up, he is beginning to think of himself in a broader and more abstract sense. He thinks of himself as a black man as opposed to the white man who exercises control over his life. Therefore he may become suspicious of Christian teachings concerning humility and regard them as instruments of control.

What political views do the elite hold? The elite are not easy to classify as conservative, moderate, liberal or radical. Almost all of the older traditional elite and some of their descendants characterize themselves as conservatives. They confess privately that they would have had the pace of advancement toward political independence follow a gradual course[13]—which would have allowed them to consolidate their social and political positions before newcomers could challenge their power and influence. But they are realistic enough to accept conditions they can do nothing to alter.

From this "old family" conservative group, too, come many of the moderates of contemporary Nigeria—persons in their forties, for the most part, who have turned from the past and look forward to the future, reasoning that "things will get better as Nigeria finds her feet." They accept the present as a transitional phase through which the country is moving; they see current problems as natural phenomena in a changing period. They look upon present political leaders as responsible and capable men who could lead the country well; but they recognize the problems created by regionalism and its divisive effect on this leadership.

The liberals among the elite are found largely in that group of persons who were youths during the days of the fight for independence when nationalism was sweeping across Nigeria. They would do away with tribal rivalry and push for "one Nigeria"; they are concerned with the need for good systems of transportation and communication, a reliable press, and selfless leadership united on the common interest. They are largely on the fringe of the very active political circles, but they participate; some of them try to educate others to the issues. As a group they are beginning to exhibit real influence where it matters most, although those among them who are high in government are generally civil servants and thus forbidden active political participation, while those in high political office are bound by party principles and programs. Almost none of them comes from old families. They are truly representative of the new day.

Having seen the general characteristics, we can now consider the classes individually. Here we start with the upper-elite class.

The Upper-Elite

This consists of the chiefs, emirs and politicians. In a society poised between two cultures, chiefs are still important in social and political life. Under military rule, after the departure of the politicians who had curbed their power, the chiefs came temporarily back into prominence; the first all-Nigeria meeting of chiefs took place in 1966 after the second military coup seemed to threaten law and order. In the North, the military rulers needed to rely on the emirs to maintain order and local government.[14]

Nigerian "chiefs" cover a wide spectrum, from the emir presiding over the government of millions of Northerners, to the village chieftain. Nor are all Nigerians who call themselves "chief" genuine rulers. For the Yoruba the title is sometimes honorific, while successful Ibos purchase their titles as a mark of dignity in later life. Chiefs in all regions, in addition to their functions in local government, gained a constitutional role in the regional houses of chiefs with the advent of parliamentary government. However, these "Upper Houses" have in practice fulfilled little useful purpose and are likely to be reformed or eliminated.

In summary, the upper-elite have a higher per capita income than any other group in the society, live in the most modern section of the cities, and enjoy all the affluence. Similar to the elite in any industrialised society, they covet power and want to continue to be its wielders. But by so doing, they occasionally lapse into spells of corruption and prestigious public spending at parties or social functions.

However shaky their position or power is now, one thing could be said about them:

They had risen to power first as visionaries and then as agitators, but independent nationhood demanded very different qualities.

The Sub-Elite or Middle Class

Nigerians run their own administration, own and operate much of their own business and require few foreigners in the professions. This provides a growing middle class of civil servants, businessmen and professionals. As we noted in a previous chapter, it has begun to show class solidarity and to become a cohesive factor in politics.

Perhaps among this class, the most like the British are the well paid senior civil servants. They have taken over the urban houses of their British predecessors in the regional capitals. In their offices, they have adopted a traditional routine much marked by its Britishness. They play tennis, and though they do not go as far as going to the beach or riding or going out in a motor boat on Sunday, they prefer to call on friends and talk politics or simply to sleep.

Within this class also are the young graduates who are new comers to the labor market and small-scale entrepreneurs as well as young executives in industry. The once popular view that Nigerians did not want industrial careers was due to the way they were treated by the foreign employers. The graduates were employed in executive positions without the responsibility that goes with such positions. The reason was the fear by the foreign personnel that if the Nigerians were allowed to understudy them, they (foreign personnel) would become redundant. This is changing because the young enterprisers are beginning to constitute a force in dynamic change—especially through small-scale enterprises and also through government policies.

The Working Class

The working class living style was described in Chapter II when we talked of the migrant in the city. Their grievances, briefly dramatized in the 1964 general strike, included the relentless fall of real wages, the low-income housing, archaic conditions of service and wage differentials based on the concept of colonial days. The Lagos consumer price index rose about 20 per cent in the first six years of independence; the rise was even steeper in Enugu (the Eastern capital), while the upheavals of 1966–70 made food in all areas soar beyond well known limits. Union pressure had, in 1963, led to the appointment of the Morgan Commission—comprising a judge, a chemist, a lawyer, an economist and a civil servant—to enquire into wages and conditions of service among junior employees. The commission concluded that for a worker with one wife and two children to live decently in Lagos he would need to earn $61 a month.[15]

The Morgan Commission also stressed the absurdity of wage differentials, which constituted an economic wonderland. A university lecturer—expatriate or Nigerian—gets roughly the same salary as his counterpart in Britain and perhaps two-thirds of the salary earned by his American colleague, though Nigeria's per capita income, at around $90,[16] is only a twelfth of Britain's and one twenty-fifth of America's. A Nigerian permanent secretary or a cabinet minister might earn $9,000 a year, plus important perquisites in the form of housing subsidies, car loans, free telephone and other services. In contrast, a laborer may earn $215. The ratio between the earnings of a laborer and those of a permanent secretary, between 1:30 or 1:40 in Nigeria, is about 1:12 in Britain and about 1:15 in the United States.[17] Fringe benefits which further widen the gap include mileage allowances and the provision of furnished houses at very low rentals. It has been calculated that about $18,000,000 is annually locked up in motor loans advanced by government.[18] If half of that were used to provide an efficient public transport system, most of the car loans would not be needed.

The Morgan Commission also found it "unfair, unjust and immoral" that large numbers of workers, including many who had seen more than ten years' continuous service, were still employed as daily-paid labor and therefore deprived of security of tenure, dismissal notice, leave pay, retiring benefit and sick leave. The Commission also attacked the exploitation of rents.

The trade unions have so far achieved little for Nigeria. Their basic handicap is that, although they have about a million nominal members, they represent only about 2 per cent of the population, while the entire wage-earning class is probably not more than 4 per cent. Chronic unemployment further weakens the unions' bargaining strength. The widespread tendency of unions to split into factions, each with its own foreign affiliations, has also hit Nigeria hard. The unity of action displayed in the 1964 general strike was a glorious exception.

Unemployment has been the result of rural-urban migration, that is, the drift to town of people from the rural areas. This obviously should be regulated and brought back to proper proportions. Now the government is begining to encourage the move back to land of the vast numbers of unemployed and uprooted workers in the town.

It is doing this by means of resettlement schemes, the development of rural housing, and villagisation-programs. However, the flood of migration cannot be halted without the free cooperation of the people themselves. So in the light of true development this free cooperation seems a very vital point. It becomes necessary that the worker takes his own responsibility or is educated to take it. There are education programs geared to foster this responsibility in workers.

With regard to factionism among unions, the greatest good will come in the field of industrial relations when trade unions can sink their differences to form a united and responsible national front. If trade unions all over Nigeria would give such a national body executive powers, then an alternative might have been found to the preponderance of weak mushroom unions which are puppets in the hands of employers. Such a national front could be sufficiently strong financially to employ skilled advisers and to use its influence to deal with recalcitrant employers. It would also be in a position to acquaint itself with the economic problems that face Nigeria.

VI
THE EFFECTS
OF INDUSTRIALIZATION
ON THE TRADITIONAL NIGERIAN
SOCIETY—A COLONIAL ASSESSMENT

Reading through the study, one will realize the many effects which have taken place as a result of the European-Nigerian contact. The first important effect is on the gradual change of the traditional value system, beliefs and religion. The introduction of monetary economy (even though it is easy to cavil today because of the slow rate of economic development during the half-century of colonial rule) replaced the trade-by-barter type of economy which traditional Nigeria was used to. Nevertheless, the difference between the condition of Nigerian (African) society at the end of the nineteenth century and the end of the Second World War (when Nigerians began to take over control) is staggering. The colonial power provided the infrastructure on which progress in the "independence" period has depended: an entirely new administrative machine, reaching down to the village in the most remote areas; a network of roads and railways; and basic services in health and education. Nigerian export of primary products brought considerable wealth to the people.

Industrialization also has resulted in individualism unknown to traditional Nigeria. Group consciousness which was characteristic of Nigeria is being replaced by the desire of independence and the assertion of individual right and freedom most evident among the young high school graduate immigrants in urban centers.[1] Although familiar attachments are still common in urban areas, yet these are found mostly among the illiterate migrants or the seasonal workers.

It seems individualism and the desire to be independent is leading to intergenerational conflict because the literate migrant is no longer willing to depend on his parents, who probably may be illiterate and therefore less understanding of the urban complexity, for decisions and guidance.

Ascription and paternalism which were highly characteristic of traditionalism are being replaced with the achievement motive and the process of competition. This shift from traditionality to modernity, as seen in Chapter I, has diminished respect for age, and has led to both public and private criticism of nepotism and tribalism. Instead of ascription, achievement tests have now been designed for selection especially into the public service and industry.

Industrialization has also led to the adoption of common attitudes. Nationalist movements are concomitants of industrialization and it is these movements that have brought about the Nigerian independence, the common citizenship and intertribal leadership which has committed itself to the task of modernization and development.

Religious institutions also played a major role in modernizing or changing Nigerians' traditional values.

In southern Nigeria, "nominal" Christians now constitute three-quarters of the population. The churches have become institutionalized. They offer avenues whereby men, who would by their age or other criteria be ineligible for traditional political offices, can achieve prestigious positions in their communities.

Missionaries introduced the Western script and made it possible for Nigerians to learn Western values which have been the impetus behind industrialization and modernization. By the introduction of Western education, the missionaries created the nucleus of an elitist class which is growing today as education improves and becomes more universal. Christianity eliminated pagan practices like twin-killing and also introduced monogamy in place of polygamy, even though the latter is still more prevalent.

Islam too has been gaining converts in the coastal areas. Today there are as many Muslims as Christians among the Yoruba. Yet Islam is for these simply a personal faith; the Yoruba kingdoms have not become theocratic states like the emirates. Nor has Muslim law ousted Yoruba customary law in any sphere, least of all in marriage, as shown in Chapter I when describing the Yorubas.

Islam has appeared more tolerant of indigenous social structure—though, at the present time, its adherents appear more strongly opposed to participation in traditional rituals or secret associations than do most Christians.

In the discussion of changing family relationships in Nigeria, achievement has been stressed in two senses. First, the relationships between husband and wife and between parents and children in the educated home may promote, in the personality of the children, a much stronger drive to individual achievement.

Extended family ties are still very strong although nuclear families are becoming gradually common, especially in the urban areas. The extended family is sometimes seen as enforcing conformity upon its members, as discouraging change. This is perhaps most marked in peasant societies, where sons follow the occupation of their fathers, and the stratification of society is seen as immutable. But we have already seen that in Nigerian tribal societies, men born to humble farmers could become wealthy and powerful men as traders or chiefs; their own children, however, could not inherit such status but had to make their own way in life. Modern society has merely provided new roles in which the traditional striving for wealth and power may be expressed.

The marriage institution is one of the many social institutions severely affected by industrialization (colonialism). K. A. Busia commenting on the colonial effect on the African marriage institution writes:

> The change from a small-scale to a large-scale social structure is having a revolutionary effect on urban marriage in its legal, economic, as well as conventional aspects. The tension is more noticeable in towns, where there are general complaints about the instability and the high cost of marriage.[2]

Customary marriage payments are still made, but the amount is usually higher, and the price of clothing and other gifts has also risen.

Statistical data could not be given to illustrate the instability of marriage, as no records are kept of marriages and divorce under native customary law. Among the reasons suggested for instability are:

1. The housing shortage.
2. Intertribal marriages often tend to be unstable since the partners often feel attachments to different tribal areas. There is little personal relationship between their respective families and there are occasionally differences in language and custom. Difficulty occurs when the two tribes have different laws of inheritance; but this cannot arise very frequently, since we are told in another context that "some" of the tribes are matrilineal. We have to realize that intertribal marriage is a result of industrialization and urbanization for as people converge in an urban center they tend to interact with themselves and hence intertribal marriages.
3. The conflict between the practice of polygamy and the newly introduced ideal of monogamy. Native law and custom permit polygamy, while the provisions of the marriage ordinance do not, and it is illegal for a man marrying under the ordinance to have another wife or wives under customary law.
4. The conflict of traditional loyalties with the European ideal, which strengthens the bond between husband and wife at the expense of kinship ties. As most of the society is patrilineal, the husband and wife owe to their separate patrilineages separate sets of obligations. Again a man's property is inherited under native law by his children and not by his wife.[3] Wives in consequence have a sense of insecurity and this is one reason why many engaged women prefer ordinance marriages, which give them and their children official inheritance, although in practice they may be forced by their husbands' relatives to fight expensive legal battles. The result is, then, the "family system," which in the old situation was a stabilizing influence keeping the married couple together, becomes a disrupting influence in the new.

With regard to stratification, few West African societies are, however, completely egalitarian and Southern Nigeria can be counted among the few, while Northern Nigeria may be excluded. In the precolonial era domestic slavery was practiced in both North and South Nigeria, and slaves (particularly in the North) were generally ineligible for political and ritual office, though in some centralized states (like the Yoruba kingdom) the slaves of kings and chiefs were granted titles and wielded considerable power.

Although there is a sort of egalitarianism now in Nigeria, yet within this egalitarian framework it is possible to create differences of wealth and political power (as shown when discussing the "elites"), and the gap between the income of rich and poor is greater than that now current in industrial societies. Craftsmen are poorly remunerated for their work. The wealth of the farmer derives in the main initially from his hard work, together with some skill in assessing the potentiality of local soils and climate. In caste-like societies like the Hausa-Fulani emirates, the wealthy commoner still finds it hard to aspire to political office; for him wealth is an alternative to political office, since wealth has become a new form of motivation for climbing the social ladder.

But on the whole as far as social stratification is concerned, the European contact has led to a restratification of society. At first oppositions between traditional concepts of status and rank and those developing in urban societies were a source of conflict which might hamper social development. High status in the tribal society was greatly respected as such; but under urban conditions, achieved status in terms of Western skills and consumption patterns tends more and more to predominate; and achievement in these respects is sometimes closely associated with competitiveness, a rejection of traditional obligations, education and income. The process tends to coincide with Parsons' "pattern variables"—a shift from traditional to modern, a clear evidence of social change or modernization.

Rural-urban migration has also affected the traditional system. It has led to a loosening of the urban immigrant's ties with the primary group. While to a certain extent it emancipates him, it temporarily restricts his participation in social life. It means that he is enrolled in and attached to an artificial "patchwork" community where, in view of his precarious social position, his role during the period of adaptation bears no relation to that which he played in his earlier coherent and stable group. His resultant feeling of isolation is accompanied by a sense of insecurity, due to the relaxation of the traditional social supports and controls. It is further accentuated by the daily need to grapple with diverse problems in an unfamiliar social setting whose administrative structure, because it is not easily comprehensible, he tends to regard as threatening or arbitrary.

Urban migration has led to unemployment and destitution for many immigrants are unable to find employment. (The number of unemployed is not given because of lack of statistics.) Those who have friends or relatives remain in town to be fed and clothed by them, thus helping to lower the general standard of living. Some even live below the level they were used to in the rural communities. Unemployment is a new concept for, in the traditional era, communal work on farms used to employ everybody. But industrialization has resulted in individual efforts to go ahead. Housing problems, overcrowding in cities, and secondary associations like occupational, tribal, social and recreational associations, trade unions and political associations are all new to the urban town-dweller. These are all the products of industrialization. Traditional Nigerian society was only used to primary associations.

Heterogeneity, a common process in urban centers, has led a modern Nigerian into face-to-face relationships with his ethnic fellows and strangers from within and without, for every large center has a quarter inhabited by strangers who have come as traders or petty craftsmen.

With regard to politics and authority, the policy of the British government toward her colonies contains contradictions. The British sought to develop indigenous African institutions, the logical result of which would have been to devolve power upon a legislature of traditional rulers; yet they trained an executive class to work within Western-style bureaucracies, so encouraging these men to aspire to higher offices than the colonial government was prepared to grant. The subsequent frustration gave birth to the nationalist movements. Industrialization opens up a wide spectrum of job opportunities and job specialization unknown to traditional Nigerian society.

Such a transformation has altered the old power relations and the traditional status system. As often pointed out, in societies which were once hierarchical, rank and power no longer coincide. Barring an adaptation of the "chief" to new economic conditions (e.g., the Yorubas), and societies which one might describe as exhibiting "egalitarian tendencies" (e.g., the Ibos) possibilities for personal advantages develop at the same time as magic observances called forth by jealousy at the refusal of inequality. Customary honors and positions of importance are explained by reference to a precise social system, based upon the sacred character of the chief or the elder; the new political relations reveal the determining and the brutal role of the economic conditions introduced by the colo-

nial power. Any authority exercised over an individual tends to
lead to the use of this individual as a producer of wealth; in such a
case the relations between different generations, between sexes, and
between unequal members of the same society become undefined.
Every exploitation of one of the channels of the circulation of
wealth has tended to become a continual accumulation of goods
and capital, which is then being put to usurious use. The deteriora-
tion of the system of exchange of women (and of commodities of
higher value which are treated in an analogous fashion to women)
can be explained as a result of this double tendency.

Moreover, the introduction of bureaucracy has led to leadership
conflict. The Western-educated elite have taken over the leadership
of the people, and to forestall the traditional rulers, (the chiefs and
emirs) from rebelling, they have attempted to include these traditional rulers in the government through political appointments to
the House of Chiefs. This strategy by the elitist class tends to pacify
the traditional rulers.

But in examining the impact of the colonial period on the Nigerian tribal societies, least change seems to have occurred in the
Hausa-Fulani emirates, where the native authorities closely follow
the traditional units. The British retained the autocracy of the emir,
and though his subordinate chiefs were made heads of administrative districts instead of holding dispersed fiefs, his control over
them was little modified. This pattern is however changing fast.

Another new phenomenon is the specification needed for political leadership. In early phases of Westernization political leadership was commonly expected from any of the few educated
Africans, but today professional politicians have emerged. Western-style political movements are also consciously attempting to re-
establish links between urban and rural areas on a new territory-
wide basis.

Colonial rule resulted in the rise of the elitist class—the Western-
educated—and this was due to the establishment of schools which
provided clerks for the civil service, catechists and teachers for the
missions, and a few men who became independent professionals.
Many of these, and especially the more highly educated among
them, lived in the colonial capitals and through the nationalist
movements sought to wrest power from the expatriate rulers. And
in so doing they identified themselves more with the entire colonial

territory than with their own ethnic groups or local communities. Today they are still the forerunners of modernization, but there are some among them who feel that Western influences have made the African lose his identity. Therefore, the fundamentalists among the "elite" want a revival of traditional African ways of doing things. The progressive thinkers among them want a modification of the good traditional values in the light of the modern. So among the "elite" there are differences in ideologies, both social and political.

It is with this relatively small Western-educated elite that the future of Nigeria depends. For this elite now wields political power. It is the innovating group responsible for mediating between European and traditional African values. The rate of economic development will, to a large extent, depend on the ability of the new leaders to seize the opportunities open to them.

Colonialism (industrialization) has led to a lot of changes originating within industry. Deviations from older patterns have taken a number of forms within the more recently established or expanding industrial organizations. Expatriate professionals and artisans have been imported to direct the new technical operations and to supplement manual skills insufficiently available in the local population. Thus, more intimate and relaxed interpersonal relations, especially between Africans and imported Italian workers (working in the construction industry), are in some cases introducing a great measure of interracial solidarity.

The implication of changes in the working situation for other relationships are profound. Acceptance of overriding claims of economic development has enabled industry to some extent to cut across the informal values and established expectations of members of the society by importing European skilled manual workers. This has not only resulted in a reallocation of task within industry but has also made it possible for other European workers of a similar social type to be brought into increasing use in commerce and in the public services, and has eased the way for the further importation of whatever type of labor will most effectively serve economic ends.

Thousands of newcomers of all races brought in by industrial development are, it is true, being indoctrinated with the standardized, stereotyped racial valuations and beliefs. Impressions gained within the work situation are carried out into other spheres of the urban society and even further afield. But at the same time industry is also producing some situations which fail to fit existing formulas and challenges many existing theories of the Nigerian society.

On the whole, from a society with a closed economy, characterized by its limited extent and the strict control exercised over the production and circulation of goods, the Nigerian society is changing into a society whose economy is open, sensitive to the vicissitudes of the exterior market, and permits an accumulation of capital inconceivable within a traditional framework. This is a process of transformation from an agricultural society with a loosely knit population and a decentralized administration to a society in the process of industrialization, in which this process together with the centralization of power by the colonizer favors the rapid growth of an urban population; from a society limited in its relations with the exterior world to one in which the methods and the frequency of communications are being multiplied and accelerated.

Nevertheless, the traditional systems of social structure, most of them based on a farming economy, continue to operate among the vast rural majority. Moreover, these systems still condition the attitudes of the new migrants to the towns. But the direction of social change is irreversible and the spread of education and the pushing of modern means of communication into the remotest areas must inevitably bring into being a modern, presumably Westernized, type of society.

I have attempted to present in a nutshell some of the disruptive and constructive social aspects which the process of industrializing Nigeria has brought about. Most of the points raised here obtain in many other developing nations which are in the process of industrialization. As noted in the introduction, I have limited the problem to a narrow perspective to enable me to handle it realistically. There is still a lot to be done in the whole field of the effects of colonialism with its by-products of industrialization, Westernization, and urbanization on former colonial states.

I NOTES

1. UNESCO, Social Implications of Industrialization and Urbanization in Africa South of the Sahara, *The International African Institute*, London, 1956, p.47.

II NOTES

1. National Economic Council, "The Development Plans of the Governments and Statutory Bodies and the Financing of Them," *Economic Survey of Nigeria*, 1959 (Lagos, 1939), Chapter II.
2. H. H. Smythe, *The New Nigerian Elite*, Stanford University Press, Stanford, California, 1960, p. 173.
3. W. A. Lewis, "The Economic Development of Africa" in Calvin W. Stillman, ed., *Africa in the Modern World*, University of Chicago Press, Chicago, 1955, pp. 97–98.
4. H. H. Smythe, *op.cit.*, p. 69.
5. U. S. Army, *Area Handbook for Nigeria*, Second Edition, March, 1964, p. 129.
6. *Ibid.*
7. *Ibid.*
8. *Ibid.* See Chapter 2, Historical Setting; Chapter 6, Social Structure; Chapter 11, Religion; Chapter 21, Political Dynamics.
9. *Mallam* is a teacher of the Moslem religion, Islam.
10. U. S. Army, *op. cit.*, p. 130.
11. K. S. Carlston, *Social Theory and African Tribal Organization: The Development of Socio-Legal Theory*, University of Illinois Press, Urbana, 1968, pp. 157-161.
12. *Ibid.*, Chapter 8, "The Ibo," p. 190.
13. S. Ottenberg, "Ibo Receptivity to Change," *Continuity and Change in African Culture*, eds., W. R. Bascom and M. J. Herskovits (Chicago, 1959), pp. 136, 138.
14. S. Ottenberg, "The System of Authority of the Afikpo Ibo in Southeastern Nigeria" (Ph.D. Thesis, Northwestern, 1957), pp. 349, 258–259, 297, 351, 85–86, 351, quotations at 347, 354–355; M. Green, *Ibo Village Affairs* (London, 1947), pp. 88–89. See R. A. Levine, *Dreams and Deeds: Achievement and Motivation in Nigeria* (Chicago, London, 1966), which is concerned with Hausa, Ibo, and Yoruba.
15. U. S. Army, *op.cit.*, Chapter 6, Social Structure.

16. The Yoruba Kingdom was in existence long before the coming of the Europeans. They had a king, courtiers and advisors. It was a form of government.
17. K. S. Carlston, *op.cit.*, pp. 181–188.
18. U. S. Army, *op.cit.*, p. 131.
19. *Ibid.*, p. 132.
20. K. S. Carlston, *op.cit.*, Chapter 9, pp. 211–237.
21. Mallory Weber, "Individualism, Home Life and Work Efficiency Among a Group of Nigerian Workers," *Occupational Psychology*, 1967, 41, 183–192.
22. Hans Wolff, "Intelligibility and Inter-Ethnic Attitudes," *Anthropological Linguistics*, March 1959, 34–41.
23. H. H. Smythe, *op.cit.*, p. 158.
24. H. H. Smythe, *op.cit.*, p. 158.
25. K. S. Carlston, *op.cit.*, pp. 213–214.
26. Harold I. Gunn, "Pagan Peoples of the Central Area of Northern Nigeria," *Ethnographic Survey of Africa, West Africa*, Part 12, Daryll Forde, ed., International African Institute, London, 1956.
27. Cf. K. S. Carlston, *op.cit.*, pp. 167–214; Harold I. Gunn, *op.cit.*, Part 12; U. S. Army, *op.cit.*, pp. 165–168.
28. Harold I. Gunn, *op.cit.*, Part 12; U. S. Army, *op.cit.*, p. 160.
29. J. O. Lucas, *The Religion of the Yorubas* (Lagos, 1948); E. B. Idowu, *Olodum are: God in Yoruba Belief* (London, 1962); D. Forde, "The Yoruba Speaking Peoples of Southwestern Nigeria," *Ethnographic Survey of Africa*, D. Forde, ed. (London, 1951), West Africa, Part IV, 1–10; P. C. Lloyd, "The Yoruba Lineage," *Africa*, XXV (1955), p. 234.
30. See K. Buchanan, "The Northern Region of Nigeria: The Geographical Background of Its Political Duality," *The Geographical Review*, XLII (1953), p. 451.
31. The reasons why the above mentioned tribes are oriented toward Western-style enterprise have been mentioned previously—these reasons are due to the achievement motive inherent in the Ibo culture and tradition, their receptivity to change and their fluidity of nonautocratic political organization. Cf. S. Ottenberg, *op.cit.*, pp. 136, 138.
32. P. C. Lloyd, *Africa in Social Change*, Penguin, 1967, pp. 101–102.
33. Stillman, *op.cit.*, p. 89.
34. *Oba* means a chief or king in the Yoruba language.
35. K. S. Carlston, *op.cit.*, Chapter 7, The Yoruba, pp. 177–189.
36. H. H. Smythe, *op.cit.*, p. 68.

37. U. S. Army, *op.cit.*, pp. 174–176. See also E. A. Ayandele, *The Missionary Impact on Modern Nigeria, 1842–1914: Political and Social Phases,* Longman, London, 1960.
38. K. S. Carlston, *op.cit.*, pp. 167–170.
39. *Emir* is a Moslem leader. He has both religious and political powers.
40. U. S. Army, *op.cit.*, pp. 168–174.
41. *Jihād* is the campaign which Muslims should wage against unbelief (and unbelievers). "Community" is a translation of *jamā'a'*, the usual Arabic and Hausa term for the followers of Sheikh.
42. M. Last, *The Sokoto Caliphate,* Humanities Press, New York, 1967, p. 228.
43. Except Silame, rebuilt some twenty years later.
44. M. Last, *op.cit.*, p. 230.
45. J. R. Ayoune, "Occidentalisme et Africanisme," in *Renaissances,* Special number, October, 1944.
46. Leopold S. Senghor, *On African Socialism,* Praeger, New York, 1964, pp. 72–73 (translated by Mercer Cook).
47. Leopold S. Senghor, "Constructive Elements of a Civilization of Negro-African Inspiration," *Presence Africaine,* Vol. 24–25, 1959.
48. K. S. Carlston, *op.cit.*, Part 3, Nigeria.
49. J. Greenberg, "Islam and Clan Organization Among the Hausa," *South-Western Journal of Anthropology,* III (1947), p. 193.
50. U. S. Army, *op.cit.*, p. 113.
51. P. C. Lloyd, *op.cit.*, pp. 171–192.
52. W. B. Schweb, "Kinship and Lineage Among the Yoruba," *Journal of the Royal Anthropological Institute,* 1 (New Series, 1966), p. 484.
53. P. Bohannan and G. Dalton, *Markets in Africa,* Anchor Books, Doubleday and Company, Inc., Garden City, New York, 1965, pp. 130–179.
54. U. S. Army, *op.cit.*, p. 114.
55. U. S. Army, *op.cit.*, pp. 115–116.
56. Eileen Jensen Krige, "Changing Conditions in Marital and Parental Duties Among Urbanized Natives," *Africa,* IX (January, 1936), 1–23.
57. *Ibid.*
58. *Ibid.*, p. 1.
59. *Ibid.*, p. xvii.

60. Cf. Richard C. Thurnwald, *Black and White in East Africa* (London: George Routledge and Sons, 1935), pp. 108ff.
61. See Louis Wirth, "Urbanism as a Way of Life," *American Journal of Sociology*, XLIV (July, 1938), pp. 1–24.
62. *Ibid.*, p. 13.
63. Krige, *op.cit.*, pp. 18–19.
64. U. S. Army, *op.cit.*, p. 124.
65. In the French original the dominant foreign minority is called "Société Coloniale." These terms are explained further in Georges Balandier, "La Situation Coloniale: Approche Théorique," *Cahiers Internationaux de Sociologie*, Vol. XI (1951). In order to avoid misunderstanding, the term Société Coloniale has been translated as "Foreign elite" and the term Société Colonisée as "native society."
66. K. S. Carlston, *op.cit.*, Part 3, Nigeria.
67. See C. K. Meek, *op.cit.*, pp. 53–58; P. C. Lloyd, "Agnatic and Cognatic Descent Among the Yoruba," *Journal of the Royal Anthropological Institute*, 1 (New Series, 1966), p. 484.
68. S. F. Nadel, "The Kede: A Riverine State in Northern Nigeria," *African Political Systems*, M. Fortes and E. E. Evans-Pritchard, eds. (London, New York, Toronto, 1960), pp. 177–178.
69. U. S. Army, *op.cit.*, pp. 106–107.
70. C. F. Meek, *op.cit.op.cit.*, pp. 197–200.
71. K. S. Carlston, *op.cit.*, p. 195.
72. H. H. Smythe, *op.cit.*, pp. 90–91.
73. *Ibid.*, p. 90.
74. In an effort to develop uniform standards of skill at various levels of proficiency, the federal government has developed a series of trade tests covering a great variety of occupations. See U. S. Army, *op.cit.*, p. 216. Also, Mallory Weber, *op.cit.*, pp. 185–186.
75. H. H. Smythe, *op.cit.*, pp. 65, 173.
76. *Ibid.*, p. 65.
77. P. C. Lloyd, *op.cit.*, p. 272.
78. Sir Henry Willink, Colonial Office, Nigeria. Report of Commission appointed to inquire into the fears of minorities, p. 11 (hereafter called Minorities Report), 1958.
79. H. H. Smythe, *op.cit.*, pp. 102–106. Also see Walter Schwarz, *Nigeria*, Pall Mall Press, London, 1968, pp. 19–23.
80. F. Harbison, et al., *Industrialism and Industrial Man*, Oxford Press, 1964. "The logic of industrialization" means that all roads lead to industrialization for it is the inevitable phase of

mankind. It carries with itself its own logic—some social institutions and behavioral patterns are required. So all industrial societies are going to end up being similar.

81. Robert A. Levine, *Dreams and Deeds: Achievement Motivation in Nigeria*, The University of Chicago Press, Chicago and London, 1966, pp. 78–79.
82. D. Scibel, "Some Aspects of Inter-Ethnic Relations in Nigeria," *Nigerian Journal of Economic and Social Studies*, Vol. 9, No. 2, July, 1967.
83. Everett E. Hagen, *On the Theory of Social Change*, Dorsey Press, Homewood, Illinois, 1962.
84. *Ibid.*, p. 185.
85. L. J. Lewis, et al., *Society, School and Progress in Nigeria*, Pergamon Press, Oxford, New York, 1965, p. 20.
86. A. V. Murray, *The School in the Bush*, Longmans, London, 1929.
87. W. T. Morrill, "Immigrants and Associations: The Ibo in the Twentieth Century Calabar," *Comparative Studies in Society and History*, No. 4, July, 1965.
88. Robert A. Levine, *op.cit.*, p. 89.
89. *Ibid.*, p. 90.
90. W. T. Morrill, *op.cit.*, p. 447.
91. W. R. G. Horton, "The Boundaries of Explanation in Social Anthropology," *Man*, XLIII, 1963, pp. 10–11.

III NOTES

1. E. F. Frazier, "The Impact of Colonialism on African Social Forms and Personality," in C. W. Stillman, *Africa in the Modern World*, The University of Chicago Press, Chicago, 1955, p. 72.
2. Louis Wirth, "Urbanism as a Way of Life," *American Journal of Sociology*, XLIV.
3. H. H. Smythe, *The New Nigerian Elite*, Stanford University Press, Stanford, California, 1960, pp. 50–51.
4. *Ibid.*, p. 51.
5. P. C. Lloyd, *Africa in Social Change*, Penguin, 1967, p. 117.
6. *Ibid.*, pp. 117–118.
7. Robert Morgan, at the Institute of Community Health, University of Lagos, is currently doing research to measure urban residential stability.

8. Max Sorre, *Les Fondements de la Géographie Humaine* (Paris: Librairie Armand Colin, 1952), III, 76 ff. For West Africa see Henri Labouret, *Fayants d'Afrique Occidentale* (Paris: Gallimard, 1941).

9. P. C. Lloyd, *op.cit.*, pp. 96–97.

10. *Ibid.*, p. 92.

11. I. Schapera, *Married Life in an African Tribe*, New York, Sheridan House, 1941, p. 132. Also see C. C. Onyemelukwe, *Problems of Industrial Planning in Nigeria*, Longmans, London, 1966: Columbia University Press, New York, 1967, p. 70.

12. See Audrey T. Richards, *Land, Labour and Diet in N. Rhodesia*, New York, Oxford University Press, 1939, pp. 383–386.

13. P. C. Lloyd, *op.cit.*, p. 100.

14. Philip J. Foster, "Status, Power and Education in a Traditional Community," in *School Review*, Vol. 72, 1964.

15. Rose Hum Lee, *The City: Urbanism and Urbanization in Major World Regions*, Chicago, Lippincott, 1955, p. v.

16. P. C. Lloyd, *op.cit.*, pp. 109–110.

17. K. M. Buchanan and J. C. Pugh, *Land and People in Nigeria*, London, University of London Press, 1955.

18. See F. A. Wells, et al., *Studies in Industrialization: Nigeria and Cameroons*, Oxford University Press, 1950, p. 30, and also Mallory Weber, "Individualism, Home Life and Work Efficiency Among a Group of Nigerian Workers," *Occupational Psychology*, 1967, 41, pp. 183–192.

IV NOTES

1. Paul Bohanan, *Africa and Africans*, The Natural History Press, Garden City, New York, 1964, p. 4.

2. 1962–1968.

3. Nigeria's Six Year Development Plan, p. 23.

4. *Ibid.*

5. Report of the Commission Appointed to Review the Educational System of Western Nigeria, Government Printer, Ibadan, 1961.

6. Report of the Commission, *op.cit.*, pp. 4–8.

7. *Ibid.*, pp. 4–8.

8. Report of the Federal Advisory Committee on Technical Education and Industrial Training, Federal Government Printer, Lagos, 1959.

9. C. C. Onyemelukwe, *Problems of Industrial Planning in Nigeria*, Longmans, London, 1966; Columbia University Press, New York, 1967. Also see U. S. Army, *Area Handbook for Nigeria*, Second Edition, March, 1964, pp. 523–524.

10. C. Aboyade, "Some Implications of Nigerian Imports Structure," *Nigerian Journal of Economic and Social Studies*, March, 1962, p. 53.

11. C. C. Onyemelukwe, *op.cit.*, p. 34.

12. Each region is free to direct its finances but it has to contribute to the coffers according to means. The amount is then redistributed according to each region's needs.

13. U. S. Army, *op.cit.*, pp. 420–421.

14. a) J. Hackett and A. Hackett, "Economic Planning in France" (Allen & Unwin, 1963); b) "Economic Planning in the Netherlands, France and Italy," *Journal of Political Economy*, June, 1960.

15. P. T. Bauer and B. S. Yamey, *The Economics of Underdeveloped Countries*, Cambridge University Press, 1957, pp. 152–160.

16. National Development Plan 1962–1968, Federation of Nigeria, Paragraph 15, p. 5.

17. Studies in Economic Development with Special Reference to Conditions in Underdeveloped Areas of Western Asia and India, Routledge & Kegan Paul, London, 1957, pp. 13–14.

18. W. B. Reddaway, *The Development of Indian Economy*, Allen & Unwin, 1962, pp. 114–115.

19. C. C. Onyemelukwe, *op.cit.*, p. 43.

20. Western Nigeria Official Document, No. 2, 1964, p. 2.

21. W. B. Reddaway, "Objectives of Indian Economy: The Objects of the Exercise Restated," *Oxford Economic Paper* (New Series) Vol. 15, November, 1963.

22. Final demand is defined as that part of the total use not devoted to further production.

23. "Objectives of Indian Economy: The Objects of the Exercise Restated," *op.cit.*, p. 59.

24. U. S. Army, *op.cit.*, pp. 421–422.

25. C. C. Onyemelukwe, *op.cit.*, pp. 51–52.

26. Walter Schwarz, *op.cit.*, p. 292.

27. *Ibid.*

28. *Ibid.*

29. "Too Much Beer?", *West Africa*, February 8, 1964.

30. *The Rededication Budget*, Federal Ministry of Information, Lagos, April, 1965.

31. *Nigerian Morning Post*, April 15, 1965.

32. Controls were, however, imposed after the outbreak of the Civil War in 1967.
33. Professor Alfred Opubor, at the University of Lagos, told the author in a conversation that the newspaper at home attacked most of the foreign companies in 1969 for their unwillingness to reinvest in the country. They have devised techniques of dodging government inspection.
34. Walter Schwarz, *op.cit.*, pp. 285–286.
35. United Nations *Bulletin*, 12, New York, 1968, p. 21.
36. Allan Mountjoy, *Industrialization and Underdeveloped Countries*, Hutchinsons University Library, London, 1963.
37. P. C. Lloyd, *Africa in Social Change*, Penguin, 1967, p. 45.
38. W. A. Lewis, "Reflections on Nigeria's Economic Growth," Development Centre Studies, OCDE, Paris, 1967, p. 45.
39. F. Harbison, et al., *Industrialism and Industrial Man*, Oxford University Press, 1964.
40. Guideposts for Second National Development Plan, 1966.

V NOTES

1. Arnold J. Toynbee, *Civilization on Trial*, New York, Oxford University Press, 1948, p. 214.
2. P. C. Lloyd, *Africa in Social Change*, Penguin, 1967, p. 125.
3. H. H. Smythe, *The New Nigerian Elite*, Stanford University Press, Stanford, California, 1960, p. 44.
4. P. C. Lloyd, *op.cit.*, p. 127.
5. H. H. Smythe, *op.cit.*, p. 167.
6. U. S. Army, *Area Handbook for Nigeria*, Second Edition, March, 1964, p. 112.
7. Bronislaw Malinowski, *The Dynamics of Culture Change*, New Haven, Yale University Press, 1949, p. 25. For a criticism of the theories set forth in this book see Max Gluckman, *Malinowski's Sociological Theories*, Cape Town, Rhode-Livingstone Institute, Oxford University Press, 1949.
8. Ellsworth Faris, "Culture and Personality Among the Forest Bantu," *The Nature of Human Nature*, New York, McGraw-Hill, 1937, pp. 278–288.
9. *Ibid.*, p. 288. Also see Mallory Weber, "Individualism, Home Life and Work Efficiency Among a Group of Nigerian Workers," *Occupational Psychology*, 1967, 41, pp. 183–192.
10. Diedrich Westerman, *The African Today and Tomorrow*, New York, Oxford University Press, 1949, p. 65.

11. Edwin W. Smith, *Knowing the African*, London, Lutterworth Press, 1946, p. 65. See also L. P. Mair, *An African People in the Twentieth Century*, London, George Routledge & Sons, 1934, pp. 275 ff.
12. Diedrich Westerman, *Africa and Christianity*, New York, Oxford University Press, 1937, p. 102.
13. H. H. Smythe, *op.cit.*, p. 116.
14. Lugard was the first British governor of Nigeria who introduced the system of "Indirect Rule," that is, ruling indirectly through the traditional rulers, who were the chiefs.
15. Report of the Commission on the Review of Wages, Salary and Conditions of Service of the Junior Employees of the Governments of the Federation and in Private Establishments (The Morgan Commission), p. 20.
16. Calculations by Dr. S. A. Aluko, unpublished.
17. Walter Schwarz, *op.cit.*, p. 25.
18. Calculations by Dr. S. A. Aluko, unpublished.

VI NOTES

1. Mallory Weber, "Individualism, Home Life and Work Efficiency Among a Group of Nigerian Workers," *Occupational Psychology*, 1967, 41, pp. 183–192.
2. K. A. Busia, "Social Survey of Sekondi-Takoradi," *Social Implications of Industrialization and Urbanization in Africa South of the Sahara*, UNESCO, 1964.
3. *Ibid.*, p. 80.

BIBLIOGRAPHY

Alec, Roger. "Nigerian Workers," by Mallory Weber, *Occupational Psychology*, Vol. 41, No. 4, October, 1967.

Apter, David. *Politics of Modernization*, University of Chicago, Chicago, 1965.

Awolowo, O. *Path to Nigerian Freedom*, London, Faber, 1966.

Ayandele, E. A. *The Missionary Impact on Modern Nigeria, 1842–1914: Political and Social Phases*, University of Ibadan History Series, London, Longmans, 1966.

Azikiwe, Nnamdi. *The Development of the U. K. for the Eastern Region of Nigeria*, London, 1957.

Bascom, William R. "Urbanization Among the Yoruba," *American Journal of Sociology*, March, 1955, p. 446.

Bauer, P. T. and B. S. Yamey, *The Economics of Under-Developed Countries*, New York, Cambridge University Press, 1957.

Belshaw, Cyril S. *Traditional Exchange and Modern Markets*, Englewood Cliffs, N. J., Prentice-Hall, Inc., 1965.

Bohannan, Paul. *Africa and the Africans*, Garden City, N. Y., The Natural History Press, 1964.

Bohannan, Paul, and George Dalton. *Markets in Africa,* Garden City, N. Y., Doubleday and Company, Inc., 1965.

Bower, P. A., et al. *Mining, Commerce and Finance in Nigeria*, London, Faber, 1948.

Bretton, H. L. *Power and Stability in Nigeria*, New York and London, Praeger, 1962.

Brown, Charles V. *Nigerian Banking System*, London, Allen and Unwin, 1966; Evanston, Northwestern University Press, 1966.

Buchanan, K. M. and J. C. Pugh. *Land and People in Nigeria*, London, University of London Press, 1955.

Carlston, Kenneth S. *Social Theory and African Tribal Organization*: *The*

Development of Sociological Theory, Urbana, Chicago, University of Illinois, 1968.

Conference on the Government of African Cities, April 18–19, 1968, Lincoln University, Pennsylvania, Lincoln Department of Political Science, Institute of African Government, 1968.

Cook, Arthur N. *British Enterprise in Nigeria*, London, Frank Cass, 1963; New York, Barnes and Noble, 1965.

Cookson, John A., et al. "Area Handbook of Nigeria," U. S. Army, Second Edition, March, 1964.

Davies, H. O. *Nigeria: The Prospects for Democracy*, London, Weidenfeld and Nicholson, 1961.

Ekwensi, Cyprian. *Jagua Nana,* London, Panther, 1963; Evanston, Northwestern University Press, 1963.

Ekwensi, Cyprian. *People of the City*, London, Heinemann, 1963.

Farfunwa, A. Babs. *New Perspectives in African Education*, Lagos, Macmillan and Co., Nigeria, Ltd., 1967.

Forde, Daryll and R. Scott. *Native Economy of Nigeria*, London, Faber, 1946.

Friedland, W. H. *Unions, Labor and Industrial Relations in Africa*, Ithaca, Cornell University Center for International Studies, 1968.

Gould, Peter R. *Africa: Continent of Change,* Belmont, California, Wandsworth Publishing Co., 1961.

Gray, R. F. and P. H. Gulliver. *The Family Estate in Africa*, Boston, University Press, 1964.

Green, M. M. *Ibo Village Affairs*, Second Edition, London, Frank Cass, 1964; New York, Praeger, 1964.

Gunn, Harold. "Pagan Peoples of the Central Area of Northern Nigeria," *Ethnographic Survey of Africa*, West Africa, Part 2, Daryll Forde (ed.), London, International African Institute, 1956.

Hackett, J. and A. Hackett, *Economic Planning in France*, London, Allen and Unwin, 1963.

Hackett, J. and A. Hackett. "Economic Planning in the Netherlands, France and Italy," *Journal of Political Economy*, June, 1960.

Hagen, Everett E. *On the Theory of Social Change*, Homewood, Illinois, Dorsey Press, 1962.

Harbison, F., *et. al. Industrialism and Industrial Man*, Galaxy Books, London, Oxford University Press, 1964.

Hodgkin, Thomas. *Nigerian Perspectives*, London and New York, Oxford University Press, 1960.

Horton, W. R. G. "The Boundaries of Explanation in Soc. Anthropology, *Man*, XLIII, 1963.

Hopen, C. Edward. *The Pastoral Fulbe Family in Gwandu*, London, Oxford University Press, 1958.

Hunter, Guy (ed.). *Industrialization and Race Relations*, London, Oxford University Press for Institute of Race Relations, 1965.'

Huntington, Samuel P. *Political Order in Changing Societies*, New Haven and London, Yale University Press, 1968.

"Investment in Education," Federal Ministry of Information, Lagos, 1960.

Jones, G. I. *Trading States of the Oil Rivers*, London, International African Institute, 1964.

Last, M. *The Sokoto Caliphate*, New York, Humanities Press, 1967.

Legum, Colin. *Pan-Africanism: A Short Political Guide,* New York, Praeger, 1962.

Levine, Robert A. *Dreams & Deeds: Achievement Motivation in Nigeria*, Chicago, London, University of Chicago Press, 1966.

Lewis, L. J. *Society, Schools and Progress in Nigeria*, Oxford, London and New York, Pergamon Press, 1965.

Lloyd, Peter C. "The Yoruba Town Today," *Sociological Review*, Vol. VII, 1959. Special issue on urbanization in West Africa.

Lloyd, Peter C. *Africa in Social Change*, Baltimore, Md., Penguin Books, 1967.

Lucas, J. D. "The Religion of the Yorubas," *Africa*, XXV, 1955.

Luyembazi, Francis L. *Economic Planning and the Trade Unions in West Africa*, Free Labor World, Spring, 1966.

Mackintosh, John P., *et al. Nigerian Government and Politics*, London, Allen and Unwin, 1966.

Macmillan, W. M. *Africa Emergent,* Pelican Books, Middlesex, Harmondsworth, 1949.

Mair, Lucy. *The New Africa,* London, C. A. Watts and Co., Ltd., 1967.

Meek, C. K. *Law and Authority in a Nigerian Tribe,* London, Oxford University Press, 1937.

Miner, Horace (ed.). *The City in Modern Africa,* London, Pall Mall Press, 1968.

Mitchison, Lois. *Nigeria, Newest Nation,* New York, Praeger, 1960.

Morrill, W. T. "Immigrants and Associations: The Ibo in the Twentieth Century Calabar," *Comparative Studies in Society & History,* Vol. 5, No. 4, July, 1963.

Mountjoy, Allan. *Industrialization and Underdeveloped Countries,* London, Hutchinsons University Library, 1963.

Moore, Wilbert E. *Industrialization and Labor,* Ithaca, Cornell University Press, 1951.

Murray, A. V. *The School in the Bush,* London, Longmans, 1929.

Mazrui, Ali A. *The Anglo-African Commonwealth: Political Friction and Cultural Fusion,* Oxford, London, New York, Pergamon Press, 1967.

"Nigeria," *Economic Development and Cultural Change,* Vol. 15, October–November, 1966.

Noyes, Andrian. *Volunteers in Development,* London, Overseas Development Institute Ltd., 1966.

Obi, Chike. *Our Struggle,* Yaba-Lagos, 1955.

Okigbo, P. N. C. "Nigeria National Accounts, 1950–1957," Federal Ministry of Economic Developments, Enugu, Nigeria, 1959.

Onyemelukwe, C. C. *Problems of Industrial Planning in Nigeria,* London, Longmans, 1966; New York, Columbia University Press, 1967.

Ottenberg, S. "Ibo Receptivity to Change," *Continuity and Change in African Culture,* W. R. Bascom and M. J. Herskovits (eds.). Chicago, 1959.

Phillips, Claude S., Jr. *The Development of Nigerian Foreign Policy,* Northwestern University Press, Evanston, 1964.

Raza, M. Ali. "Emerging Trade in Public Labor Policies and Union-Government Relations in Asia and Africa," *California Management Review,* Vol. 9, Spring, 1967.

Reddaway, W. B. "Objectives of Indian Economy: The Objects of the Exercise Restated," *Oxford Economic Paper* (New Series) Vol. 15, November, 1963.

Reddaway, W. B. *The Development of Indian Economy*, London, Allen and Unwin, 1962.

Report of the Commission on the Review of Wages, Salary and Conditions of Service of the Junior Employees of the Government of the Federation and in Private Establishments (The Morgan Commission), Federal Ministry of Information, Lagos, 1964.

Report of the Federal Advisory Committee of Technical Education and Industrial Training, Lagos, Federal Government Printer, 1959.

Roberts, B. C. *Labour in the Tropical Territories of the Commonwealth*, Bulletin for London School of Economics and Political Science, London, 1964.

Robinson, Ronald (ed.). *Industrialization in Developing Countries*, University Overseas Studies Committee, Cambridge, 1965.

Schwarz, Walter. *Nigeria*, London, Pall Mall Press, 1968.

Seibel, H. D. "Some Aspects of Inter-Ethnic Relations in Nigeria, *Nigerian Journal of Economic and Social Studies*, Vol. 9, No. 2, July, 1967.

Sklar, Richard. *Nigerian Political Parties*, Princeton, Princeton University Press, 1963.

Textor, Robert B. (ed.). *Cultural Frontiers of the Peace Corps*, Cambridge, Massachusetts Institute of Technology Press, 1966.

Tilman, Robert O. and Taylor Cole (eds.). *The Nigerian Political Scene*, Durham, N. C., Duke University Press, 1962.

United Nations. *Bulletin*, 12, New York, 1968.

UNESCO. *Social Implications of Industrialization and Urbanization in Africa, South of the Sahara*, London, The International African Institute, 1956.

Warren, W. M. *Urban Real Wages and the Nigerian Trade Union Movement, 1939–1960*, Chicago, The University of Chicago Press, 1960.

Weber, Mallory. "Individualism, Home Life and Work Efficiency Among a Group of Nigerian Workers," *Occupational Psychology*, 1967, 41.

Wells, P. A. and W. A. Warmington. *Studies in Industrialization: Nigeria and Cameroons*, Oxford University Press, 1950.

Wauthier, Claude. *The Literature and Thought of Modern Africa: A Survey*, London, Pall Mall Press, 1967.

Wraith, Ronald and Edgar Simpkins. *Corruption in Developing Countries*, London, Allen and Unwin, 1963; New York, Norton, 1964.

Wraith, Ronald and Edgar Simpkins. *Local Government in West Africa*, London, Allen and Unwin, 1964; New York, Praeger, 1964.

Zik: A Selection from the Speeches of Dr. Nnamdi Azikiwe, London and New York, Cambridge University Press, 1961.

INDEX

INDEX